A COTSWOLD COUNTRY DIARY

Other Publications by Barn Owl Books

Other titles by Gordon Ottewell:

A COTSWOLD COUNTRY DIARY

by
Gordon Ottewell

With a Foreword by Winifred Foley

Drawings by Aylwin Sampson

Barn Owl Books, 33 Delavale Road, Winchcombe, Glos.

First published in 1989 by
Barn Owl Books, 33 Delavale Road, Winchcombe, Gloucestershire GL54 5YL

———————————

British Library Cataloguing in Publication Data:
Ottewell, Gordon
A Cotswold Country Diary
1. England. Cotswolds. Social Life.
1. Title.
942 4'170858

ISBN 0 9510586 5 7

Phototypesetting & Printing by Higham Press Ltd., Shirland, Derbyshire

Contents

Let us get out of these indoor narrow modern days, whose twelve hours somehow have become shortened, into the sunlight and the pure wind. A something that the ancients called divine can be found and felt there still.

Richard Jefferies
The Amateur Poacher

Foreword

Ramblers through the countryside like Gordon Ottewell are a rare species. A combination of botanist, ornithologist and archaeologist, with an artist's eye and a literary pen, he pays homage in this book to one of nature's lovely areas, the Cotswolds.

One hopes that it will find a place in every urban library where it could provide in its pages a pleasant oasis for the mind of the town dweller. Here he can forget the noise of busy traffic, the glaring lights and doubtful distractions of television, and turn his mind to country things — the balm of hedgerows and meadows, streams and mossy banks, wild creatures and bird song — in the company of an author who knows and loves his subject.

Winifred Foley

Acknowledgements

I should like to acknowledge my debt to Adrian Faber, Editor of the 'Gloucestershire Echo', for so readily giving permission for the publication of these pieces, all of which first appeared in his newspaper.

I must also place on record my appreciation of the practical help provided by the Editor, and by David Leake, towards the production of this book.

My thanks too, go to Aylwin Sampson, not only for his excellent artwork, but also for much invaluable advice on the publication of the book.

I am deeply indebted to Winifred Foley for agreeing to read the work in draft form and for contributing such a generous Foreword.

Finally, I wish to extend a warm 'Thank you' to all those readers who suggested the re-issuing of 'In the Country' as a book. I trust that the finished product will bring them further pleasure.

G.O.

Introduction

I started writing my weekly country notes in the 'Gloucestershire Echo' in August 1979, under the heading 'Cotswold Commentary'. After some years this was amended to 'Reflections of a Countryman', and later to 'In the Country' — the title by which my contribution is still known. This little book represents about a quarter of the 500 or more pieces that have appeared over the ten years since then.

As the title suggests, I have restricted the collection to the Cotswolds and have arranged the pieces under eleven theme headings, rather than stick exclusively to the traditional seasonal format.

Though not a diary in the strictest sense of the word, the pieces were written as a direct result of experiences gained while exploring some part of the Cotswolds, or — in the case of the section entitled 'Chiefly Children' — through personal contact with children during my work as a head teacher in a Gloucestershire primary school.

Gordon Ottewell,
Winchcombe,
Summer 1989

To Margaret

Spring

CAPRICIOUS March has indulged in all its accustomed antics, revealing the many facets of its fickle temperament with bewildering rapidity.

Days of clear skies and warm sunshine have been interspersed with those of unrelieved greyness and driving rain. Snow showers have swept across the wolds, dispelling our complacency that winter's retreat was accomplished. And the cutting, cheek-numbing winds for which the month is especially noted have added their unwelcome contribution to the constantly changing weather pattern.

Little wonder therefore, that some of the customary signs of spring are proving slow to reveal themselves. It was not until the 22nd that I found my first clump of coltsfoot flowers, hitherto having come across only isolated specimens. Nearby, in a damp ditch, a cluster of pale pink butterburr flowers were just emerging on their stout hollow stems. These related plants both produce flowers in advance of their leaves, which leads the casual observer into imagining that flower and leaf are separate species.

In the woods, that characteristic flower of early spring, dog's mercury, was undeterred by the weather's caprice. The first tiny green flowers had emerged from their spikes before February was out, and the dark green lanceolate leaves carpet the woodland floor in many places, providing welcome evidence of the resurgence of life in the bare leafless woods.

Along the hedges, the swelling leaf buds of the hawthorn produce a green stippled effect during these days before the leaves at last burst out and unfurl their fresh greenery. Hedges lining busy motor roads are already in full leaf, thanks we are told, to the heat generated by passing cars.

Everything will come to those who wait however, and soon our Cotswold hedgerows will be things of beauty and leaf-clad mystery once more.

29 March 1980

Spring

NOW IS the time of the great unfurling, with each day seeing a new tree or shrub extending its array of freshly opened leaves to produce that unique mantle of greenery so praised by poets and keenly missed by exiles.

The tall sycamores at the entrance to the wood displayed leaves the colour of burnished copper, contrasting with the delicate green of the birches, whose slender forms swayed gracefully in the breeze.

Beneath their canopy the white flowers of the wood anemones nodded, living up to their name of wind flower. According to legend, these flowers remain open only when the wind blows. Two other country names bestowed on the wood anemone are crowfoot and smell fox. The former is obviously associated with the trifoliate divided leaves but the origins of the latter are less easily explained. Although a member of the ranunculus family — plants which include the buttercup and the marsh marigold — the wood anemone differs from most of its relatives in being poisonous, the juice from its stem causing a blistering of the skin in certain cases.

The track beneath the trees was lined with that other and equally delightful white spring flower, the wood sorrel, rising above a carpet of bright clover-like leaves on the woodland floor. This plant was commonly used as a flavouring for salads in former times, when it was often referred to as green sauce. It is also said to have had religious associations, especially with the druids, and was later known as the hallelujah plant in the Middle Ages. Legend has it that wood sorrel was the 'shamrock' used by St. Patrick to illustrate the story of the Trinity.

My discovery of clumps of primroses and a scattering of violets beneath the unfurling hazels set the seal on a happy hour's ramble.

25 April 1981

THE DAY had begun dull and cheerless, with intermittent drizzle sweeping across the wolds from a sombre grey sky.

The first gaps in the cloud sheet began to appear soon after midday however, and within an hour and a half the clouds had dispersed, the landscape was bathed in sunshine and the transformation was complete.

A solitary skylark rose from the sodden ploughland beside the wood, making up in sheer exuberance for the lack of polish in its fragmentary song. Unless winter performs a treacherous about-turn, it will have perfected its song by mid-March, when it will pour out its notes with the ecstasy for which it has long been renowned as the first light of day brightens the fields.

By contrast, all was silent within the wood. The tasselled catkins dangled motionless from the hazel twigs. No tremor disturbed the clusters of brittle bronzed leaves on the beeches. Hanging raindrops glistened like myriads of finely-threaded pearls along the lower branches of the spruces.

No movement perhaps, but abundant signs of life were everywhere evident. Emerald spikes of dog's mercury sprouted from the leaf mould carpeting the woodland floor. Tufts of fresh grass splashed colour into the cluttered ditches by the fringe of the wood. Drifts of snowdrops flecked the patches of cleared ground, and a first primrose had begun to unfurl along the hedgebank.

And now, gradually, stealthily, the birds announced their presence. On the outer limits of sound at first, their low, almost furtive notes grew steadily louder. The straining ear detected a tapping, a ceaseless industrious pecking among the dark green tresses of the spruces towering above.

Patience was finally rewarded. A fleeting glimpse of the tiny feathered bundle suspended momentarily overhead was sufficient to register the telltale white nape-patch of the coal tit, oblivious to the prying eye of the earthbound watcher as it continued its ceaseless treetop quest.

6 March 1982

4

Spring

THE RECENT rainfall served to settle the dust along the lanes and bridleways but the ridges dividing the ruts are still iron-hard, making walking difficult.

Fresh green blackthorn foliage has replaced the blossom that was such a delight along the hedges from March onwards, and the air is thick with the heavy scent of may.

The hedgerow trees are at their best by now. The newly-unfurled sycamore leaves spread a canopy of shade and the late-bursting ash provides an ideal contrast with its delicately fashioned leaflets. Several other trees and shrubs play significant roles in May's colourful pageant. Deserving of special mention are the ornate leaves of the field maple, which will make a major contribution to autumn's subtle hedgerow tapestry.

The boldy-veined leaves of the hazel too, assume a prominence now, supported on our lime-loving soils by dogwood, buckthorn, guelder rose and wayfaring tree — all combining to give a variety of shape and colour and acting as a reminder that many of our local hedges have borne witness to centuries of change across this Cotswold landscape.

Bird life abounds within the leafy labyrinth of a hedgerow in May. The practised ear can detect the presence of several unobtrusive summer migrants as well as resident blackbirds, thrushes, dunnocks and robins. Among those species favouring our local hedgerows is the skulking, sober-coloured whitethroat, whose scratchy, erratic warble is sometimes delivered as it rises from its hedgerow cover in an uncharacteristic burst of activity.

By contrast, the olive-coloured willow warbler utters its delightful cadences continuously as it searches the upper branches of the hedge for the insects upon which it feeds.

It is the occasional blackcap warbler however, that enriches our tree-lined hedgerow most, treating the discerning listener to a song of such richness of tone that at its best it may justifiably be compared with that unrivalled virtuoso, the nightingale.

29 May 1982

5

THE WINDS of March, beloved of poets and popular song lyric-writers of bygone days, maintained their chilling bluster throughout the month and, aided and abetted by cloudy skies and low temperatures, kept spring firmly in abeyance.

True, we were treated to a little fleeting sunshine, during which the greens of the landscape took on a warmer, richer appearance and a promise of better things to come. But the general air of a long slow retreat on the part of winter persisted until the month's end.

So in the absence of the awaited migrant birds, we drew consolation from the behaviour of their resident relatives. Greenfinches added their nasal twitter to the morning chorus of robin, blackbird, song thrush and chaffinch, and their less familiar cousins, the handsome lively little siskins, provided plenty of interest and entertainment in their feeding habits at the bird table and on the suspended nut-feeder.

Along the hedgebanks and by the woodland slopes meanwhile, the trailblazers among the spring flowers began to brave the inhospitable conditions and started the inexorable process of carpeting the bare ground once more. Dog's mercury, surprisingly colourful before the emergence of its competitors, gave an early lead, soon to be followed by wild arum, goosegrass, and a host of other unremarkable yet nonetheless welcome common plants.

The first splashes of cream and yellow — provided by the primrose and lesser celandine — had appeared by the middle of the month to delight the eye and to soften the starkness of the scene, while by the roadside, pushing through the detritus of winter, bold yellow coltsfoot heads added their gaudy share of welcome colour.

Above, in the hedges, the hazel's tossing catkins lost their striking freshness with each passing week, and we needed to turn to the first white clusters of blackthorn blossom for assurance that spring was indeed on its way at last.

7 April 1984

Spring

HOW WARMLY I agree with the Cotswold writer whose book began with the words: 'The bare trees and windswept fields of March reveal the structure of a countryside more clearly than one can ever discover it in leafy June'.

With the morning sunshine beckoning through the leafless branches, I took the old lane and was soon climbing steadily towards the escarpment. The last grey traces of snow were gradually thawing, adding their share to the network of tiny streams flowing down the slope, fed by a cluster of springs, making the going heavier the further I climbed.

What better reason could there be for increasing the frequency and duration of stops as the view began to open out below? For with no foliage to impede the gaze, it soon became possible to take in a fine sweep of scenery away to the west, dominated by the great upthrust of Bredon Hill, with its scattered outliers adding their distinctive shapes to the scene.

Closer at hand, the patchwork of fields, woods and snugly-nesting farmsteads took on a bloom of warmth in the sun's brightness, while the towering beech trunks overhead revealed an ever-changing pattern of shade and texture as the sun's rays freely penetrated the canopy of bare twigs and branches.

What green there was to be seen near at hand was provided almost exclusively by ivy. Its shiny, densely-packed leaves carpeted the woodland floor, cushioned the decaying tree stumps and clad the older trees with a luxuriance that no other plant can match.

Here and there however, signs of new spring growth were emerging. The merest suggestion of goosegrass, the first hints of cow parsley, the bolder spikes of dog's mercury. While at intervals along the way, the bright green arrows of unfurling wild arum leaves confirmed that spring was indeed advancing, soon to clothe the muted scene with its mantle of fresh colour.

And as I reached a clearing high on the hillside, a sprinkle of snowdrops provided a delicious foretaste of that coming treat, when the bare bones of the landscape will be enveloped once more in the verdure of spring.

22 March 1986

ONE CONSOLATION for the disappointing weather throughout much of early April has been the delight of renewing acquaintance with the songs of migrant birds as May's promise approached.

An early-morning cuckoo provided a cheerful and evocative start to a late April day — after the chiffchaff, my first summer visitor.

A blackcap's rich, casually delivered notes added genuine bird music to the resident chorus of blackbird, song thrush and chaffinch. Blackcaps remain as residents in the locality in increasing numbers nowadays, but the likelihood is that wintering birds move northwards as spring approaches, to be succeeded by migrants from the south.

But it was the first tentative notes of the tiny willow warbler that my ears were straining to detect as I followed the winding lane along the woodland fringe and which I finally tracked down in a clump of ancient hazel coppice. No bird song possesses quite the same kind of enchanting subtlety as this delicate cascade, delivered time and time again by the insignificant olive-green warbler. Both blackbird and blackcap possess superior power and variety of song but the willow warbler remains my favourite herald of the delights of early summer.

Identifying bird song is guaranteed to sharpen the senses, but even the experts are occasionally taken in by bogus sounds. The story goes that a famous ornithologist once followed a mysterious call-note for the full length of a bushy hedgerow before discovering that he had been keeping pace with a man pushing a creaking wheelbarrow on the other side of the hedge.

This story served as some consolation recently when I too was deluded into thinking that I had heard an unfamiliar bird sound. Driving along a country road with my window down, I heard above the engine a strident sound not unlike the scolding notes of certain birds. I pulled onto the verge and switched off the engine. Sure enough, the sound was repeated at regular intervals — too regular, in fact.

A search along the roadside hedges revealed nothing however. Looking up, I at length discovered the source of my 'bird call' — the movement of overhead power cables caused by maintenance work nearby.

10 May 1986

Spring

PERHAPS the most exasperating occupational hazard faced by the country diarist is the sudden change of weather that so often takes place almost immediately after the writing of a supposedly topical piece.

Our capricious climate, as though determined to live up to its notorious reputation, has a disconcerting habit of lulling one into thinking that a settled spell is likely, only to betray our trust with little or no warning and plunge us back into starkly unseasonal conditions.

This week however, having delayed putting the finishing touches to a piece on signs of the advance of spring, I am prompted to temper my exhuberance by glancing through the window at a landscape once more blanketed with snow.

Not that this recent development in any way nullifies the pleasure gained from sights and sounds appropriate to the advancing year. I had discovered my first lesser celandine, heard my first full-throated songs of the mistle thrush and skylark, and seen my first black-headed gulls in full breeding plumage before February was out.

And before winter staged its unwelcome revival, March had brought the first pure white flowers on the cherry plum in the hedgerow, the first sustained outburst of blackbird song in the garden, and on a lighter note, the first precocious lawn mower out for inspection from within a suburban garage!

Meanwhile, the newly-emerged elder leaves in the hedgerow are covered in a chilly layer of snow, the lesser celandines have disappeared from view beneath the same white mantle, and the garden birds have been driven once more to resort to picking up a living from household scraps, while the gulls, hungry but wary, sweep low over the houses before making off to forage further afield.

The future outlook therefore, appears decidedly bleak but knowing the wiles of this unpredictable climate of ours, life could well have returned to normal by the time these words appear in print.

14 March 1987

MY DESTINATION was the vast Iron Age hill fort, perched high above the village, but as usual my readiness to be sidetracked ensured a few extra delights to compensate for the climb.

A meagre tally of butterflies during April and early May prompted me to keep a lookout for new species as I left the village and skirted a cornfield on the lower slopes of the hill. Sure enough, I obtained my first success on the weedy fringe — a small copper, basking in the afternoon sunshine, its unmistakable orange and brown colouring rendering it conspicuous against a comparatively featureless background.

Woodland flowers in turn provided plenty of interest as I climbed beneath a dappled canopy towards my destination. The bluebell carpet though fading slightly by now, still cast its blue haze under the phalanx of tree trunks, but my interest soon turned to the woodruff's white stars, the gaudy splashes of newly-unfurled red campion, and the bugle's distinctive erect stems.

Beyond the last trees, with the outer ramparts of the hill fort visible now ahead, a pause to regain breath was pleasantly filled by gazing back over the treetops the way I had come, taking in the richness of the scene as this south Cotswold landscape faded away in the haze of a May afternoon.

Gaining the fort at last, I paused to watch a cuckoo beating its way between the treetops below before setting off to walk between the ramparts of this 32-acre relic of man's endeavour in pre-Christian times.

I had not gone far before spotting another new butterfly on the ground before me — this time the tiny, unobtrusive grizzled skipper, which soon disappeared as my shadow fell upon it. There was still another species of butterfly to reward my climb — a small heath, which in characteristic fashion closed its wings immediately on landing. In good butterfly summers, small heaths are the walker's constant companions over grassland from May until mid-August.

If this small heath proves to be the first of many I encounter this summer I'll be more than delighted.

23 May 1987

Spring

INSTEAD of following the bridleway as it climbs beyond the hedged fields and begins its ascent of the open hillside, I opted for what seemed the easier route along the tiny valley.

Although shielded from the wind's blast and spared the gruelling climb, I soon discovered my lowland route had its share of hazards. The tiny stream had carved itself a steep-sided gorge, the spongy banks of which provided unstable walking, necessitating a cautious and tiring descent, made even more difficult by the decaying trunks of long-dead trees lying across the path at intervals.

More of these fallen giants littered the flank of the hillside away to the right, their bleached, shattered forms encrusted with leathery fungi, their severed stumps almost concealed by cushions of luxuriant moss. Lower down the deeply-gouged valley, bright green thongs of hart's tongue fern sprouted from the damp shady ledges, providing a gaudy contrast to the muted shades of decay which otherwise dominated the surroundings. No bird called here and no precocious spring flower bloomed.

It was with some relief that I reached the lower path skirting a clump of woodland and began the undulating return route back to the junction with the bridleway. Soon, the last of the dead trees were left behind and their place taken by plantings of healthy timber — a mixture of conifers and deciduous trees, with a fine stand of wild cherry predominant.

Now too, the birds and animals missing on the early part of my walk seemed determined to make amends for their absence. The lusty calls of a great tit echoed through the well-budded branches, a wren stuttered into activity from the depths of the tangle of bramble, and well-fed rabbits bounded for cover between the array of tree trunks.

My path passed close to a clearing in which sedges fringed a shallow pond. Here, lesser celandines starred the fresh grass and the first shoots of great willow herb were beginning to push their way through the mat of lower vegetation.

Already the valley of dead trees was receding from memory — crowded out by these signs of burgeoning spring growth.

19 March 1988

11

A Cotswold Country Diary

Summer

A FINE morning beckoned, and my dog and I rose early. The drone of a distant combine harvester, proof of an even earlier riser, was the only man-made sound as we climbed the slope above the village and looked down on the valley below — still silent and partly hidden in the morning mist.

Snails were everywhere in the damp vegetation, their multicoloured shells adding to the variety of tints provided by the roadside flowers — the pinks and reds of knapweed, restharrow and willow herb, the blues of cranesbill and scabious, and the yellows of lady's bedstraw, agrimony and ragwort.

Moths added their subtle colouring to the picture as they rested motionless on the stems and flowers and a solitary green-veined white butterfly clung limply to a grass blade.

The birds are largely silent at this time of year. The excited chatter of hawking swallows high above and the monotonous cooing of our local pair of collared doves were the only avian sounds to be heared in the village.

A yellowhammer sat at his song post in a roadside bush on the hillside, uttering his repetitive late-summer fragment of song at intervals, and a pair of bullfinches whistled softly to one another from a blackthorn thicket close by.

My dog's interest lay in other matters and I soon became aware of the reason for his excitement. An unmistakable stench hung heavily in the air — evidence that a fox had passed that way recently on an early-morning foray.

25 August 1979

Summer

THE CLEAR skies and warm sunshine of the last few days of August saw the corn harvest in full swing. The drone of combines could be heard right round the clock, the lanes have been congested with tractors hauling their precious loads from the fields, and now the skies are being darkened by spiralling clouds of smoke as the straw is burnt in readiness for the plough.

Most Cotswold farmers take the precaution of ploughing around the margins of their fields before setting fire to the straw and stubble. A minority still fail to do so however, and the sad spectacle of a blackened, burnt-out hedge is the result. This is particularly regrettable as our hedgerows, for centuries one of man's greatest beneficial influences on the landscape, have never been so vulnerable as at the present time. Grubbed up and ploughed out by the mile to expedite higher farming efficiency, our remaining hedges need instead to be conserved not only because of their unique role as wildlife habitat but also in the interests of both farmer and gardener. Hedgerows provide shelter for livestock and serve as a deterrent against soil erosion; their value in aesthetic terms as a feature of the countryside is immeasurable.

My own garden hedge, planted about seven years ago, is thickening well now. Predominantly hawthorn, but with a few bushes of blackthorn, field maple, dogwood and wayfaring tree, plus a sycamore which is being allowed to grow into a full-sized tree, it serves as an impregnable barrier to grazing animals, a refuge to several species of song birds and wild flowers, and as a pleasing background to the garden itself.

8 September 1979

15

BIRD SONG declines both in variety and quality as July succeeds June.

Young birds assume their independence and the demands of parenthood decrease, so there is less need for the proclaiming of territories. So one of the delights of the first half of the year becomes a memory of the past.

I rose early one morning in late June, determined to savour once more the pleasure of the already dwindling dawn chorus. The morning was cool, with a fresh breeze stirring the leaves of the aspens by the bridle path. There had been heavy rain overnight and although dawn had broken fine, a few tattered remnants of sombre-looking cloud hovered around, as though threatening to inflict further rain on the already damp fields.

My destination — a low-lying copse by a little brook — loomed into view ahead in the grey dawn. A few desultory notes from a blackbird, perched in the topmost branches of an ancient willow, heralded my arrival. A chaffinch too, greeted the new day with customary gusto while distant woodpigeons added their drowsy contribution to the early morning sounds.

Welcome though these songs were, it was in the hope of hearing another less-predictable songster that I had left my bed at this unearthly hour to plod through wet grass to this particular spot. I waited beneath the caterpillar-riddled hazels by the edge of the wood, listening for the first few faltering notes that would indicate the bird's presence.

A straggling family of long-tailed tits provided a pleasant diversion, moving nimbly through the ash and willow canopy, assiduously searching for food.

And then, suddenly yet unmistakably, came the sound I had waited to hear. Casual, diffident at first, the notes soon assumed their rich resonance as the blackcap announced his presence in tones of haunting beauty.

My dawn vigil had been worthwhile.

5 July 1980

A SHORT drive over the wolds on a warm July evening quickly dispels any fear that our insect population is tottering on the brink of extinction.

Moths of every imaginable shape and size dance in the tunnelling beam of the headlights. Many, sadly, are drawn to their doom, others are stunned and left littered along the road, to fall victim to cars or to opportunist predators.

The majority however, flutter away into the scent-filled night, making the most of the hours of darkness, taking their fill of nectar before seeking suitable daytime shelter.

Compared with their relatives the butterflies, moths are often dismissed as somewhat unexciting, even dull creatures, prone to inflicting serious damage both in gardens and wardrobes, and with the disconcerting habit of entering houses on warm summer evenings to beat senselessly around electric lights.

Yet we need merely to take the trouble to examine the pathetic remains of tattered wings trapped on radiator grills, windscreen wipers and headlamp casings on the day following an evening drive to discover that the charge of dullness at least is patently untrue.

For contrary to popular belief, some of our common moths possess a range of colours and markings comparable in subtlety with those of many butterflies.

Further evidence of this often overlooked beauty can be obtained by seeking and studying moths in repose on walls, trees, fences and other surfaces during daytime. Unlike their day-flying relations, moths settle with their wings folded horizontally, revealing their structure and markings to good effect. Discovering and identifying them soon confirms that their beautiful names — burnished brass, angle shades, pale tussock, yellow underwing, rosy rustic — are well justified.

Prominent among the moths are of course the hawks — fine, strong-flying insects with ornately tinted wings. A neighbour recently showed me my first of the year — a poplar hawk, originating no doubt from the avenue of poplars nearby.

23 July 1983

UNDETERRED by the intense heat of the late afternoon, the swifts screamed in great arcs round the church tower. Their short time with us will soon be over, irrespective of the weather, and their strident urgency seemed undiminished in the wilting heat.

Earlier in the day, before the heat had intensified, a song thrush had broken the silence with a few bars of song. This repetitive outpouring will be of intermittent frequency from now on until the tuning-up process is resumed in the weeks leading up to Christmas.

These July days in fact mark the beginning of the comparatively silent period in the song-bird calendar, as young birds are successfully fledged, territorial disputes subside, and the annual moult gets under way.

Notable exceptions to this pattern are two pairs of relatives — two buntings and two doves, all of which produce familiar sounds which can charitably be termed songs, and which persist with varying degrees of polish throughout the month.

The buntings — corn bunting and yellowhammer — may lack the grace of movement and variety of song associated with their relatives the finches, but their presence cannot fail to brighten a July ramble. Corn buntings, with their dapper appearance and monotonous jingling song, are often the only bird to be seen and heard amid the ripening corn of the dipslope fields in summer. Yellowhammers can be relied on to provide a welcome splash of colour, as well as a few lethargic notes, across the wolds well into August.

The two doves — the woodpigeon, or ring dove, and the stock dove —will continue to add their own modest contribution to the muted bird chorus throughout the month.

Together with their smaller relatives, that comparative newcomer, the collared dove and the migratory turtle dove, they will help to ensure that July, the quiet month, is not altogether silent.

21 July 1984

ONCE every season, the county cricket eleven play a one-day match on a tiny, tree-fringed ground in the north Cotswolds.

The fact that this fixture was arranged for the last day of August seemed sufficient to give it the kiss of death this summer but amazingly the weather relented and an absorbing afternoon's cricket ensued.

Enjoying the sunshine and atmosphere as much if not more than the game itself, I found myself recalling the few yet memorable occasions in a village-cricket boyhood when the local side entertained a county eleven. These were of course friendly matches, more often than not benefit games for long-service county players, and we boys would queue for what seemed like hours, not only for autographs but merely to gape in open-mouthed admiration at our flannelled idols.

The games themselves were usually lighthearted affairs, with the professionals enjoying a carefree knockabout and the result seldom if ever in doubt. But to a young boy it was all a very serious matter and the thrill of fielding a ball on the boundary and self-consciously throwing it to the waiting fieldsman was undoubtedly the highlight of the afternoon.

Despite its tranquil rural setting, our annual limited-over match is no rustic romp of the kind dredged up from my boyhood memories. This was a keen, competitive game, with every run fought for and every wicket earned. For league points are at stake here as at any match played on the regular county grounds and frivolity has no place in the event.

Yet there were a few lighthearted moments to savour, such as the friendly bantering between a well-known test player and a section of the crowd whenever he moved to a fielding position within earshot. He even sat briefly with a few spectators at the fall of a wicket, which to my surprise prompted the attention of only one juvenile autograph hunter.

Country cricket, whatever the degree of accomplishment of the players, never fails to provide an absorbing pageant of delight for the watcher. And on this occasion, the constantly-changing cloud patterns, the vying sounds of distant trains and combine harvesters, the sleepy cooing of woodpigeons and the tireless darting of hawking swallows, provided endless diversions for anyone who, like myself, sees the game as a symbol of a way of life rather than as a battle for league points and table places.

13 September 1986

IT WAS oddly reassuring recently, when out on a country ramble with a group of children, to notice that the common poppy has lost none of its appeal to the young.

A couple of decades ago it seemed that weedkilling sprays and dressed seed had between them reduced the poppy to something of a rarity. The cornfield weed of our childhood appeared to be in danger of disappearing, leaving children with merely its paper image to be worn every November.

But we had not allowed for the sheer persistence of this favourite among childhood flowers. It took only a few farmers and local authorities to cease systematic spraying to enable the poppy to re-colonise marginal land and roadside verges and thus stage a dramatic revival. As a result, this summer has seen many Cotswold cornfields splashed with red as in days gone by.

The origins of this association between poppies and corn are so old as to be lost in the mists of antiquity. Poppy seeds have been found with grains of barley in the remains of Egyptian dynasties dating back over 4,000 years. The Assyrians called poppies 'The daughters of the field' while the Romans depicted their crop goddess Ceres wearing a wreath of field poppies.

The poppy has a long history in the annals of British folklore. Superstition had it that poppies should not be picked at harvest time, for fear of provoking storms, and this widely-held belief gave rise to such local names as thunderflower and thundercup.

The poppy was once credited with a range of medicinal powers. Culpeper, writing in the 17th century, advocated its use in syrup form to help cure hoarseness and 'to stay catarrhs and defluxions of rheums from the head into the stomach and lungs'. From Ceres onwards, the poppy's sleep-inducing properties have been widely recognised, while the notoriety of its opium-producing relative is well known.

The poppy capsule is a highly specialised seed-dispersal mechanism, distributing the dust-like seed through a ring of small holes. Which reminds me that I must take a photograph of our local poppy-spangled cornfield before the flowers lose their glory.

1 August 1987

20

CONSIDERING the uninspiring weather that has so far predominated this summer, the participants on my week's walking tour of the north Cotswolds were fortunate in having five consecutive days in which the rain relented and the sun put in a few welcome appearances.

Well-shod and equipped with weather-resistant clothing, we set off each day to discover something of the scenery, flora and fauna — and human endeavour too — that make the Cotswolds such an outstanding area of the English landscape.

Our daily routes were chosen deliberately to avoid the main tourist centres. By careful mapwork, we managed to keep road-walking to a bare minimum and except for one short unavoidable stretch, to keep off main roads entirely.

Green lanes comprised a good deal of our route, and bridleways and footpaths led us into the very heart of the region. Hedgerows, some of them ancient, were our companions as we walked for many a country mile, with their place taken by stone walls on the upland stretches.

We walked over open wold, where sheep wandered at will and cornfields stretched away to sweeping skylines. We plunged into dappled woodland, where impenetrable underwood hemmed us in on every side and tall trees towered overhead. We wandered by gurgling streams, weaving their enchanting way along narrow secret valleys.

Wild flowers graced our steps throughout. The reds, blues and purples of high summer were a constant joy — willowherbs and cranesbills, campions and bellflowers, woundworts and thistles — and hosts more.

Butterflies appeared as though by magic with the fitful sunshine —browns and skippers, commas and tortoiseshells, marbled whites and fritillaries. Day-flying moths and myriads of smaller insects filled the air.

We paused to watch a buzzard wheeling and a heron labour off on slowly-beating wings. An invisible grasshopper warbler reeled in the lee of a hillside and spotted flycatchers feasted on easy pickings beneath a sycamore canopy.

We looked at farms and cottages, at crops and cattle. There was always time, as the poet advised, to stand and stare. At times, very occasionally, we were aware of traffic buzzing along distant roads. And we counted our blessings and went on our way contentedly.

15 August 1987

Autumn

NOW IS the time of year when the brambles yield their bounty.

It is often said that the first blackberries are the best but the dry weather has ensured that these luscious fruits have lost none of their flavour, and the pickers have been out in strength, braving the thorns and enjoying their self-imposed task in the warm afternoon sunshine. The flies of course, are quick to claim their share of the feast, and the dull tinge on much of the fruit is a sure indication that they have discovered it already and in feeding upon it have spoilt its freshness.

Many other hedgerow fruits are at their best just now, and gladden the eye even if they fail to appeal to the palate. Elderberries hang in great bunches; those not picked by the wine-makers will sustain the blackbirds and thrushes in the cold months ahead.

The dull purple sloes stand out against the yellowing blackthorn leaves while along some of the ancient hedges, variety is provided by the dark unpalatable fruits of the dogwood, buckthorn and wild privet. There is a good crop of hawthorns this year and rose hips too, are plentiful. But the bright orange rowan berries have long since been plundered by the birds.

Those characteristic limestone shrubs, wayfaring tree and guelder rose, provide still more variety of colour in places, as do the deeply-grooved spindle fruits, with their bright pink tones. Occasionally we come across a veteran yew tree along a Cotswold hedge, and its deep red lantern-like fruits add a new depth of colour to the scene.

Of the non-woody, berry-bearing plants adding their share of colour to the hedgerow, pride of place should perhaps go to the woody nightshade, or bittersweet, whose berries are now turning from yellow to red, and hang in great chains on the hedges. And who can possibly omit the gaudy orange spikes of cuckoo pint, adding a touch of exotic colouring to the muted tones of the hedgebottom?

29 September 1979

Autumn

THE STRAGGLING little band of house martins passing my window on the 10th may well be the last of the departing summer-visiting birds I shall see this year.

Logging the arrival dates of these migrants, a practice I have maintained for a number of years, is a comparatively straightforward business; departure dates however, are a different matter. One is tempted to assume, especially with the early-leaving swifts and cuckoos, that a sighting, say in mid-August, is sure to be followed by others, only to discover some time later that the unrecorded date was in fact the last of the season. I make a solemn vow each year to jot down all migrant sightings as departure time draws near, but somehow never quite summon up sufficient discipline to keep a methodical record.

The range of autumn tints widens each day as the leaves of beeches, willows, hawthorns and maples change into a riot of yellow, gold, russet, bronze and crimson. The show of varying hues is augmented at intervals by patches of brilliant colour from the leaves of bramble and dock and from the stems of dogwood and willow herb. Meanwhile the last of the red campion flowers preserve a few fleeting memories of departed summer.

But for sheer glory, we need look no further than the horse-chestnut. For this children's favourite is well loved by the poets too; how apt was the description in Gerard Manley Hopkins' poem: 'Fresh firecoal chestnut falls'.

The massive lobed leaves and shiny chestnuts in their spiky cases combine to produce a range of rich, subtle tints guaranteed to delight the eye of young and old alike. The children are wasting no time in gathering their conker harvest and already the seasonal battles are under way in school playgrounds and along the village lanes. This timeless activity serves to remind us that some things at least remain constant in a rapidly changing world.

20 October 1979

THIS AUTUMN has been a good one locally for most species of fungi, none more so than for the shaggy inkcap.

This interesting fungus appears regularly at this time of year on disturbed ground but I seldom recall seeing so many inkcaps at one time. A member of the Coprinus family, which includes about forty different species in Britain alone, the shaggy inkcap grows a barrel-shaped cap, brown at the top and covered with shaggy white scales.

Later the expanding cap takes on a bell-like appearance with pinkish-brown edges. Soon the cap darkens and the parallel-sided gills begin to leak inky fluid as the spores gradually ripen from below upwards. Also known as the shaggy mane and lawyer's wig, this particular inkcap is not only edible but is considered a delicacy by discerning fungus eaters. It should be picked at the opened stage and can either be cooked with cheese and breadcrumbs or casseroled with salt and butter.

It is said that the inky fluid was once used for writing in country districts, although I should imagine that it was a lengthy and messy business collecting sufficient inkcaps for that purpose.

Another edible fungus plentiful this year has been the handsome parasol mushroom. This species is one of our largest British fungi, with a cap measuring up to eight inches across. Parasols prefer an open grassy situation, though can be found frequently in woodland clearings or near to clumps of trees. The fringed, scaly brown cap often stands almost a foot from the ground but the chief distinguishing feature is the ring under the cap.

Fear of poisoning prevents many people from sampling the delights of edible fungi, although few of us can resist the appeal of a field scattered with the distinctive white domes of the familiar field mushroom.

3 November 1979

Autumn

THE FIRST widespread and severe frost of the season was accompanied by patches of milky-white mist, which lay in splayed-out fingers along the narrow valleys dissecting the wolds.

The air was clear and keen, and every roof and gable sparkled in the morning light. Cobwebs festooning the hedges were delineated in perfection and even the shrivelled forms of thistles and burdocks scattered along the matted verge took on a certain statuesque silvery dignity, which remained until the climbing sun finally dispelled the last remnants of frost.

Following as it did upon several days of squally rain and inhospitable, buffeting wind, a mid-October afternoon of mellow, glowing sunshine provided a welcome uplift of the spirits. The trees were still, and the distant rolling landscape was bathed in a warm golden light, revealing every subtle detail of farm, field and hedgerow under a cloudless sky.

Yet despite the warmth and tranquillity of the atmosphere, we inhabitants — human and animal — are well aware that such a day is but a brief interlude, a temporary respite in the inexorable approach of winter. It is a day to savour, to make the most of, yet one in which to prepare for more rigorous times ahead. And so, each village garden is a scene of quiet purposeful activity. It is a time for tidying up and storing away, ready to withstand the ravages of winter. The morning frost has already withered the tips of the less-hardy shrubs and bushes, allying itself with the wind and rain in the common assault on the summer greenery which will culminate in the denuding of our vegetation as winter sweeps in to usurp autumn's brief reign.

The birds too, are preparing. Our swallows have departed for another year and winter flocks of chaffinches and yellowhammers comb the fields, soon to be joined by parties of immigrant fieldfares and redwings, as the colder, shorter days loom ahead.

24 October 1981

27

A SEA OF creamy mist filled the valley one morning recently, upon which floated the scattered crowns of a few ashes and sycamores.

All other low-lying features were obliterated from view, making the hillside ridge beyond the valley appear like a distant promontory, combining with the slope on which I stood to create a sweeping bay, with a chequered pattern of fields descending to the edge of the white expanse.

The illusion faded quickly as the sun rose, promising yet another golden September day. Soon the swallows and house martins climbed in agitated clouds from the wires along the lane, weaving intricate designs high above and as yet revealing no inclination to depart on the long and hazardous migration flight which must inevitably take place within the next few weeks.

Meanwhile in the garden the butterflies responded to the sun's irresistible prompting. Small tortoiseshells filled the air in the quest for nectar and soon the sedum blossom was covered with their colourful forms as, together with the whirring-winged silver-Y moths, they feasted with complete absorption throughout the day.

Yet despite the intensity of the sun's warmth, unmistakable signs of the advancing year encroached on the consciousness. Blackberries swelled to succulent ripeness along the hedges, hawthorns had begun to don their many-coloured autumn coat, crab-apples splashed their mature hues along the bridleway, and sloes added their sombre purple tints to the September pageant.

The swifts and cuckoos have already gone, their urges unaffected by such minor considerations as a brief extension of summery warmth. Other migrants are also on the move, as was indicated by the brief snatch of song from the tiny greenish-brown bird which alighted briefly in the garden to search a rose bed before moving on. Its short utterance revealed it to be a chiffchaff, seeking sustenance on its southward passage to distant shores.

25 September 1982

THE OCTOBER sun, which had revealed the subtle autumnal beauty of the wolds in full measure in the early morning, brought even greater delights as the day neared its end.

Late afternoon had seen a sheet of rain cloud spread across the western skies, only to be torn apart and dispersed by a lively breeze. Soon, the sun reappeared to spread its radiance across the tattered cloud formation, suffusing its warmth across each dark expanse with a network of flame-red, and etching the distant masses with a smouldering glow.

By now the vast kaleidoscope of the heavens was a riot of colour, as orange succeeded burnished gold, only to be itself eclipsed by the deepest crimson. By contrast, the overhead sky had become one of pure duck-egg blue, fading to the gentlest tinge of cream, while wispy strands of high cloud took on the appearance of yellow ochre, interspersed with a shadow as of molten lead.

Such transient splendour lasted all too briefly, however. Soon the vivid hues lost their lustre, the uniform rose-pink that then held sway fleetingly faded, and the sombre pall of evening spread across the sky. But although the pageant of colour had vanished from the skies above, the western horizon remained a blaze of glory for some time later. I was able to climb the ridge above the village and enjoy the spectacle of a rim of distant wold capped by layer upon layer of glowing colour, each brilliantly distinct — the whole topped by a sweep of purple cloud awe-inspiring in its immensity.

The last fiery vestige of sunset had been almost extinguished by the time I descended the lane towards the lights of the village. An early star appeared in the darkening heavens and a tawny owl's first wavering hoot echoed from the distant woods.

15 October 1983

THE MORNING rain clouds have passed and now watery sunshine has emerged to brighten the autumn scene, accentuating the mosaic of colour on the woodland floor.

Not that all the leaves are down yet. A tattered remnant of the woodland canopy still remains, muted in tone but resisting for a little while longer the inevitable fall. This word of course, is used by the Americans to describe autumn — and aptly so, especially just now as the downward drift nears completion and winter's ascendancy seems close at hand.

But this afternoon there is still the residue of last summer's foliage clinging to the twigs. The leaves of the beeches in particular, are a feast for the eye — their greens, golds and browns blending to lend a warm glow to the wood. The ash leaves, by contrast, appear drained of colour as they float to earth in clusters. Many break their fall by settling in the shrubs and bushes of the understorey, where their pale, feathery shapes mingle with the reds and browns of maple and hawthorn.

Underfoot, decay is already at work. The tang of rotting leaves and timber prickles the nostrils. Here in the depths of the wood, working relentlessly on the decaying stumps and long-severed boughs, a host of fungi — soft and dome-shaped, leathery and strap-shaped — thrive in the damp half-light.

Alongside the grassy sward, remnants of the ranks of flowering plants that spangled the way with colour earlier in the year can still be found. Herb Robert and red campion, woundwort and willow herb —pathetic reminders now of the glories of the departed summer.

But even here, in the very heart of the wood, the sun's autumnal rays contrive to make light, literally, of the worst that decay can do, casting an aura of mottled beauty on the scene, and keeping wintry thoughts at bay for a little longer yet.

17 November 1984

MY HILLTOP vantage point provided me with a clear view across the valley.

Late-September sunshine bathed the scene in mellow light and I found myself warming to the sentiments of such writers as D. H. Lawrence, who expressed the view that September is the best of all the months.

Scarcely a puff of cloud intruded in a sky of an intense blue rarely seen during a lacklustre summer. Few leaves were as yet on the turn and fewer still littered the grass where I walked. An Indian summer about to surprise us perhaps — it was tempting to speculate.

But the robin was not deceived. Already his notes had taken on that icy, wistful tinkle that heralds the coming of autumn. Perhaps the snatch of late chiffchaff song from the hawthorn scrub below was a parting gesture after all, and the swallow's fleeting dip beyond the ash crowns merely a wave of farewell.

But now a black cloud sweeping low over a freshly-ploughed field below caught my attention. With smooth deliberation it spread itself like an immense fan over the tilled earth before swirling suddenly to reveal a contrasting white pattern dazzling in the clear light. The lapwings — 200 at least — finally settled and were instantly lost on the dark uniformity of the ploughed field. Occasionally a bird moved, revealing a white patch. Otherwise no trace of the bird cloud could be seen.

Suddenly, without warning, the birds were airborne once more. A man with a dog was skirting the field along the footpath and the lapwings, ever restless and wary, were on the move. Backwards and forwards they flew, dividing then uniting, beating the air in their characteristic manner, crying mournfully.

I now realised that they were not alone. As is often the case, a scatter of jackdaws had joined their ranks and their raucous notes, together with the plaintive calls of the lapwings, mingled with the fairy bells of a charm of nearby goldfinches and a solitary robin's autumn soliloquy.

10 October 1987

A Cotswold Country Diary

NOVEMBER began misty but fine, with a hopeful hint of fleeting sunshine to follow — ideal conditions in fact, for a morning in the woods.

Along the approach road, the tatty mottled sycamore leaves drifted down, augmenting the underfoot carpet of ash leaves and twigs, always among the first to fall. The hawthorns too were losing their leaves, although a good crop of berries ensure that these bushes will retain some colour well into the winter.

It was in one such bush that I located a tribe of goldcrests — those engaging dwarfs of the bird world that make the tits appear almost medium-sized in comparison. My attention was attracted by their persistent twitter and as is customary with their race, they allowed me to make a close approach without showing any apparent concern. I stood for some time watching their ceaseless activity a few yards away yet was never able to obtain more than a fleeting glimpse of one particular bird.

The goldcrest was generally known as the gold crested wren in my schooldays and I was led to believe that its distribution was confined more or less to coniferous woodland. Increasing familiarity with the species over the years has revealed wider preferences however, and this little group of five or more in the wayside hawthorn seemed oblivious to the presence of large clumps of larch and spruce nearby.

Indeed, it was the dull gold of the turning larches that greeted me as I entered the woods. These tall sentinels — the sole representatives of the conifer family to lose their leaves in autumn —stood in their gilt splendour alongside mutli-coloured beeches, while beyond, a few veteran birches provided subtle contrast with their fast-diminishing pale yellow tresses.

Amid this climate of change, where the greens of summer were so rapidly losing their supremacy to the browns and golden-yellows of autumn, one tree stood unaffected by such seasonal fluctuations. Tall, bushy and with foliage of the deepest green, the old yew drew the eye from a great distance. Approaching closer, I discovered the warm glow of its mass of tiny lanterns — berries deadly to humans but precious sustenance to the birds.

Suddenly the morning's first hesitant rays of watery sunshine penetrated the dwindling canopy of the wood, turning the drifting leaves into a cascade of pure gold.

14 November 1987

Winter

PERCHED as it is on a flank of the wolds, our village took the full brunt of the recent battering winds and driving rain which swept across the country.

A torrent of muddy water surged down the hillside, clogging the drains and swirling across the road, flooding the hollows and leaving the footpaths awash. The receding water left behind a deposit of fine grit and mud, which was flung in all directions by passing traffic, while below in the village, where the road descends to the valley floor, the way was littered with small branches and twigs wrenched from the nearby trees.

Now is the time when the stark leafless hedgerows yield their once-hidden secrets. An array of birds' nests are revealed among the bare branches, ranging in size from the substantial structures of song thrushes and blackbirds to the small flimsy nests of dunnocks, finches and warblers. The snug little domed nest of a wren catches the eye, low down in a tangle of ivy close to the garden gate, causing me to wonder how I could possibly have missed finding it earlier in the year.

Not far away, high in an ash tree, the large, elaborate nest of a pair of magpies is now fully revealed. The builders managed to rear a full brood this year, supplementing their diet with eggs stolen from a nearby smallholding, where poultry still range freely. The saying 'An eye for the main chance' could well have been coined with the magpie in mind, for few creatures have developed opportunism to such a fine art as this wily thief.

Of all the familiar resident birds, it is the song thrush that I feel most indebted to at this time of year, for it is his early-morning song that has cheered us during these dark days before Christmas.

22 December 1979

34

Winter

THE FROST'S subtle artistry is revealed the moment we open our bedroom curtains on these cold, sharp January mornings. Sadly however, our senses are not at their most appreciative state so early in the day.

Fortunately, the beauty of this handiwork is not confined to the intricate etchings on window panes. Every twig, every blade of grass, is transformed, and such commonplace sights as a fallen branch, a lump of stone — or a clod of earth even — take on a new and unfamiliar appearance under their sparkling mantle.

My dog loves these frosty mornings. He bounds gleefully over the frozen turf, thrilling to the tang of scents in the keen air, and rolling over and over in ecstasy, as though determined to savour to the full every sensation the tingling morning offers. While my own interest is absorbed in the frost's accentuation of the grain on a gatepost or the pattern etched on a frozen hoofprint, his zest for life knows no bounds and it is clear that he shares my reluctance as we finally turn for home.

By now the sun, which rose in a fiery glow over the frozen fields, is beginning to make its presence felt. Its winter strength will be insufficient to penetrate the sheltered white margins of the fields over the hedge, which have retained the frost of two mornings past, but already the gleaming rays have thawed out the glittering layer on the brambles alongside the footpath and the uncovered leaves shine with water droplets in the warming air.

And now the landscape, once frozen into immobility, has suddenly come to life. A magpie wheels chattering over the hedge and a family of starlings, speckles brilliant in the sunshine, swish overhead in urgent flight.

19 January 1980

FEBRUARY has so far lived up to its fill-dyke reputation. The low-lying fields in the valley resemble a morass — even the stony footpaths and bridleways on the flanks of the ridge are standing in water.

Today however, the sun has asserted itself and has bathed the sodden winter landscape in warmth. Vast mountain ranges of cumulus cloud have rolled majestically across a blue sky, the squally, buffeting wind has given way to a gentle breeze, and we are being treated to a foretaste of spring.

In the garden, the signs of renewal are increasingly evident. Lush tufts of fresh growth appear as though by magic along the hedges and borders. Snowdrops push through the dark damp soil. The feeling of expectancy, vaguely hinted at before, is now a reality. There may be periods of severe weather ahead but the great awakening has begun.

The resident garden birds are attuned to the change. Both song thrush and robin were in good voice early in the morning and their chorus was joined by the 'Teecha, teecha' of the great tit and the spirited little refrain of the blue tit. A distant mistle thrush, perched high on the topmost bough of a tall ash, added his contribution — a sound that rises above the wind's bluster. This handsome thrush is well named stormcock — his melodious song reaches its peak as the March winds sweep across the wolds.

The sun's rays seem to bring the limestone walls to life too. Rosettes of lichens encrusting the honey-coloured stone stand out in rich contrast to the mossy mats nearby. An intrepid bee — my first sighting of the year — alights momentarily on the stone's timeworn surface — yet another harbinger of warmer days ahead.

16 February 1980

36

IN CONTRAST with the previous day, when a cheek-numbing wind had swept across the wolds, the last Sunday of the year proved to be mild and sunny, prompting people to leave their firesides to enjoy the spring-like weather along the lanes and bridleways.

Apart from the gaudy blotches of colour provided by a few scattered rose hips, the subdued shades of the season held sway along the hedgebanks. These ranged from the dark greens of ivy and bramble to the lighter, softer shades of moss and of the occasional shoots of precocious spring leaves pushing their way up well ahead of their expected time.

The purple veil that appeared to be masking a length of distant hedgerow proved on closer inspection to be rank upon rank of spiky dogwood shoots, bestowing a welcome smudge of colour. The bright sunlight also enhanced the patina-coated surface of the ash trunks further along the hedge, lending them a subtle beauty I had somehow missed on countless other occasions when walking this way.

As I reached the open ground beyond the sunken lane, the rich brown of the new ploughing glinted dazzlingly in the sunshine. These ancient fields descend in a sweeping arc into the valley, each enclosed in its own distinctive shape by its own hedge — leafless, trimmed and compact. These old hedges have parcelled out the landscape for centuries and have mercifully been spared at a time when we are losing our old hedges at an alarming rate.

High above, rooks soared and tumbled in a clear sky, their deep calls interspersed with the higher-pitched garrulous chatter of the jackdaws, rising alongside. On a lower plane, midges too, danced in the warm air, while in the far distance a kestrel hovered on outspread wings.

The afternoon was far spent as I retraced my steps between the silent hedges. The sun had sunk low in the west and a calm had settled on the fields as though to usher in the fast approaching dusk. I was to be treated to one last diversion before reaching home however — a band of twittering yellowhammers suddenly appeared, bringing a flash of warm brown and gold to the pale-pastel winter scene.

3 January 1981

ALTHOUGH the valley was completely submerged beneath a blanket of fog, the sun shone from a clear sky on the flank of the hill, causing the frost to sparkle and filling the air with an exhilarating keenness.

Every tree and bush, every branch and twig even, was a thing of rare and transient beauty in the still morning air. Indiscriminately, the frost's artistry had transformed the bleak wintry landscape into a world of fragile delight. Spiders' webs hung like silver hammocks from the hawthorns and brambles. Along the hedgerow, each upright spike of last summer's dock and hogweed was delineated to perfection by countless glistening crystals.

Overhead, a straggling flock of fieldfares exchanged rattling call-notes over the whitened fields. Closer at hand, smoke-grey woodpigeons rose with a clatter from the frosted stubble and made off with flashing white wing-bars towards the silhouetted fir clump beyond the obliterated valley. High above, a silver plane crossed our corner of the silent world unheard, leaving a white trail in its wake.

Trees and hedges became sparse as the ridge drew near. Barbed wire fences on uniform posts strode across the landscape with stark geometrical efficiency and crumbling vestiges of wartime buildings served as a grim reminder of a critical period in our country's recent history.

Yet even here the frost's handiwork was evident for all to see. Each regimented post, each rusted strand of wire was etched and decorated —transformed briefly into a fragment of a fairyland scene.

Soon the sun — part creator of this world of beauty — began the rapid and inevitable process of destruction. As I descended to the village a steady beat of water droplets sounded on the glistening leaf-strewn verge.

14 February 1981

Winter

AFTER battling through the snow out of sheer necessity on the three previous mornings, it was distinctly pleasant to amble leisurely over the white expanse, savouring to the full the transformation that had taken place across the Cotswold countryside.

Sunshine beaming over snow-blanketed fields provides a lure that many of us, whatever our age, find hard to resist. Shouts of delight echoed from the sloping meadow as the sledge skimmed over the glittering surface, while down in the village, wrapped and muffled figures wielded shovels or plodded determinedly along the snow-filled lanes, capturing something of that inexplicable satisfaction that comes from contact with our familiar surroundings after the first significant snowfall of the winter.

Like a skilled craftsman, the snow fashions the landscape with subtlety and precision. Far from casting a featureless mantle over the ground, a heavy snowfall produces a world of light and shade, a land of bold contrasts and sensitively-indicated detail. Sharp, jagged edges are moulded and softened. Less distinctive features are skilfully emphasised.

The ridge and furrow of the ancient ploughland, scarcely visible to the casual eye except when the sun sinks low on the western horizon, now appears as a bold corrugation on the slopes across the little valley.

The solitary yew, normally a somewhat incongruous addition to the clump of mixed woodland on the flank of the slope, emerges now as a strikingly distinctive feature — a centrepiece jewel in an array of sparkling gems.

Leaving the fieldpath, where the footprints of others who came this way earlier stood out in crisp detail, I strode off over the fields. Before very long I came upon the evidence I was seeking — tracks and trails of a host of tiny animals and birds that had risen early, not as I had done — for pure pleasure — but to search for some kind of sustenance along the hedges. Scratchings and burrowings, strewn leaves and split shells — telltale signs of a frantic effort to survive in a hard, wintry world.

19 December 1981

ALTHOUGH much of the snow that blanketed our low-lying areas has now disappeared, the thaw in the uplands has made comparatively little impression as yet.

This is particularly noticeable as we climb the winding lanes that pick their unpredictable way from the valley floor towards the ridge which forms the watershed between our two local river systems.

Sunken between steep hedgebanks, these ancient lanes bore the full brunt of the wind's handiwork and were soon rendered impassable by great sweeping snowdrifts. Even now, despite hours of sunshine and the efforts of snow ploughs and tractors, discoloured expanses of packed snow, topped by successive frosts, continue to hem in the traveller on either side, making hazardous any deviation from the narrow cleared path.

It is difficult to imagine, while negotiating these tortuous slopes, that the fresh new greenery everywhere apparent in the valley below was equally in evidence here before winter launched its belated offensive. Unfurling clusters of wild arum leaves had appeared along the barren hedgebottoms a short time ago, together with a sprinkling of other early growth. They have been hidden from view completely now but they will recover in due course from this unseasonal setback.

For the birds however, this late assertion of winter's power is a more serious matter. Lulled into a state of pre-courtship euphoria by the earlier mild weather, they have been driven to seeking sustenance where it can be found and a regular supply of household scraps has been needed to cater for a constant flow of visitors to the bird table.

Birds of prey in particular, have found survival difficult, as their uncharacteristic tameness shows. Returning from walking my dog one afternoon recently, a cacophony of alarm notes prompted me to look up towards my neighbour's roof. My gaze met that of a little owl, stoically enduring the protests of a host of equally hungry small birds.

26 February 1983

THE WEATHERMAN had predicted snow before the day was out and the cold air and grey sky above seemed to confirm the probability of the forecast.

Scarcely a leaf remained on the oaks in the spinney alongside the lane. The only sound of life was the brief high-pitched call of a treecreeper working its spiralling way assiduously up a blackened trunk, apparently managing somehow to find a few insects or other invertebrate fare to sustain its tiny frame in these unpromising surroundings.

The hedgerows flanking the lane on its twisting climb were also bereft of life for the greater part of the ascent. A solitary robin made a fitful investigation of a bramble patch, but it was not until I reached a clump of roadside beeches that any purposeful activity — in the form of a few chaffinches and a pair of blue tits — brought a sparkle of life to the brooding numbness of the afternoon.

The sky's greyness intensified as I topped the slope and began to follow the undulating road along the flank of the wooded escarpment. Not all my newly-acquired warmth was attributable to the recent physical effort, I now realised — the rise in temperature heralded the approaching snow, the first flakes of which soon began to float earthwards like thistledown, only to disappear without trace on the leaf-strewn verge.

Bird activity increased in the lee of the wood. Blackbirds and thrushes were busy turning over the leaves in the hedgebottom and a wren bustled into view from a mossy log to scold me lustily as I passed. Woodpigeons clattered from the overhanging branches to sweep in great arcs above the bare treetops.

Leaving the woods behind for the open country, I lingered to watch two coveys of partridges motionless on the arable before heading for home as the first snow of the winter began to settle over the darkening fields.

17 December 1983

THE HILLSIDE climb, a stiff test at all times, presented something of a challenge under a covering of snow.

The tyre-marks of a Land Rover carrying fodder to livestock on the upland fields served to provide some foothold at first but beyond the last gate the tracks petered out and those of a solitary sledger provided the only evidence that others had come this way. Eventually these too were left behind and I faced a vast white expanse untouched by human foot. It was time for a brief pause to steady the breathing and to contemplate the view.

Below, the little town lay enveloped in its snowy blanket, dwarfed by the sprawling woods across the winding valley. A wisp of fine mist hung above the silent streets as the grey afternoon brooded and threatened an early dusk.

Evidence of the hill's wild inhabitants was everywhere to be seen. Black cones of molehills erupted across the snow-filled fields and had clearly provided interest, if not more tangible satisfaction, to a fox, whose prints linked several hills and whose droppings had been deposited on one of the more prominent mounds.

Rabbit tracks too, were there in plenty, criss-crossing the snow from the direction of a blackthorn thicket in the hollow of the old quarry. Scratchings and scrapings appeared in sheltered places, where these hungry rodents had endeavoured to obtain food but they seemed to have had little success.

Descending the hillside by the wood, the birds' plight was clear to see. Heaps of decaying leaves by the hedge had been flung about by the ravenous blackbirds and thrushes. The hawthorn crop had been stripped from the hedges, which looked bare and inhospitable in the failing light, offering scant cover to the huddled forms of the redwings settling down to the ordeal of another hard winter night.

26 January 1985

THE WOODS were silent on a cold, sharp afternoon as the old year neared its end.

Every rut and hoof-print was layered with ice. The leafless birches stood sentinel, their silver trunks contrasting with the dull uniformity of the wall of conifers, while behind, great grey beeches towered against the wintry sky.

Sheltered beneath the depleted canopy, the ground vegetation remained surprisingly immune to the rigours of winter. Brambles, green as ever, sprawled across the path; dog's mercury, although less colourful, still carpeted the open spaces. The few berries splashed welcome colour against the sober background. Rose hips especially, stood out in vivid contrast to leafless twigs, challenged closely by rings of bright red berries of the guelder rose.

Underfoot, pale whitebeam leaves littered the path as the trees thinned out. A scattering of herb Robert flowers, undeterred by wind and frost, looked set to survive to welcome in the new year.

Still no sound broke the silence. Even that dandy of the woods, the jay, looped away without a single note of raucous protest at my presence. Scratchings of freshly-dug earth lay along one stretch of the path but the nocturnal digger had left few clues as to its identity.

Exchanging the woodland's shelter for the open common proved something of an ordeal. Penetrating wind nipped and numbed, sweeping unhindered over this upland terrain, buffeting the gorse and wrenching at the wiry scrub. A mile or so of battling against this icy blast followed before the path dipped again to pass a huddle of weatherbeaten barns and plunged back into the valley. The three venerable ashes close by the barns had taken a battering since my last visit, one having had a huge bough torn away, leaving a fresh jagged scar defacing its scaly trunk.

Back in the cover of the woods, I lingered to catch a glimpse of a pair of tiny goldcrests, whose urgent, high-pitched notes alone broke the silence, before heading homewards as the pastel-pinks of a late-afternoon sky finally blended into a dusky smudge on the western horizon.

10 January 1987

43

A Cotswold Country Diary

Wold Landscape

THERE CAN be no more evocative link with prehistoric times in this area of the Cotswolds than Belas Knap long barrow.

This vast, whale-backed earthwork, almost a thousand feet above sea level, is reached only after a determined climb and the sense of achievement on attaining this objective is in no sense diminished either by the number of previous visits or by the tell-tale evidence of other visitors' litter.

The tattered remnants of the morning's rain clouds had finally dispersed as we set off across Cleeve Common, and by the time we reached Postlip Mill, and had paused to listen to the first chiffchaff of the year jingling away unconcerned from the cover of the hazels near the mill pond, a fresh breeze had got up and the sun was making its welcome presence felt.

Early violets were in bloom by the footpath to Winchcombe, lesser celandines carpeted the banks of a swollen stream hurrying beneath the budding willows, and the laugh of a green woodpecker echoed from a distant belt of woodland.

These sights and sounds were soon left behind as we climbed the steeply-ascending path beyond Corndean Hall towards the Knap. The trees thinned out, to be replaced by wiry thickets of gorse and blackthorn and the only bird sound was that of a solitary skylark, battling upwards to deliver a persistent thread of song audible above the wind's bluster.

We paused to admire the workmanship of the restored portal and to reflect on the 4,000 years of Cotswold history preserved so uniquely at this spot. Then we continued our ramble by Wontley Farm towards the gorse-strewn expanse of Cleeve Common. Leaving the lower slopes, above which lapwings called mournfully over the dark ploughland, we were met by the full force of the wind, so that it came as something of a relief to dip at last below the craggy edge of Cleeve Cloud, with Cheltenham lying in sunny calm below.

5 April 1980

Wold Landscape

OVER THE years the stone seat half way up the hill above the village has gradually been engulfed by blackthorn scrub. Now however, the bushes have been cut back and it is possible once more to rest midway up the slope and to admire the view stretching away beyond the valley over the gently rolling wolds.

And what a view this vantage point offers, especially on an evening in early June, when the landscape basks in the soft radiance of sunshine after rain, with the tones and colours of both natural and man-made features revealed at their best. In the foreground, the ancient ribbed pastures, where cattle graze amid spangled buttercups, descend to the lower slopes, bounded by dense hedges with sentinel trees at intervals.

Beyond, the stone gables of the village houses stand out in a honey-coloured glow, behind which the silvery expanse of gravel pits in the valley catches the late sunshine. The middle distance offers a superb view of the chequerwork of field, hedge and woodland which so typifies the best in our rural landscape. Mile upon mile it stretches, limitless in its variety of shape and colour, each change in the cloud pattern above revealing fresh facets to delight the appreciative eye.

Finally the skyline itself, with its belts of corrugated woodland, isolated barns and tiny bristling trees, applies the finishing stroke of perfection to the scene.

Looking up from my notebook, I realise that during my immobile preoccupation with the view, I have been accepted as a harmless feature of the surroundings by my wild neighbours. Two rabbits nibble unconcernedly at the lush grass near where I sit, the sun's low rays accentuating the pink membrane of their raised ears. They scamper for cover as I rise from the seat — an intruder in their private world.

7 June 1980

47

THE INTERMITTENT drizzle which had persisted throughout the morning began to die out by mid-afternoon and the sun emerged to disperse the grey rain clouds and transform the rolling landscape.

Soon, vast mountains of cumulus cloud appeared, borne along like some splendid and fantastic pageant by a fresh breeze, which cleared the air, sharpened the senses and toyed with the leaves of the ash trees dotted across the fields.

By now, every gentle elevation along the road revealed new vistas of distant scenery. The patchwork of walled fields stretched away as far as the eye could see. Beyond, rising up to meet the cloudy peaks above, a majestic sweep of the Wiltshire chalklands formed an impressive backcloth to the unfurling view.

The breeze had lost none of its freshness by early evening but the cloud mass had rolled away, leaving merely a few isolated wedges of sombre purple cloud, dispersed in a sea of clear, steely-blue sky.

As sunset approached, the western horizon was filled with a suffusion of pale orange, fading to primrose yellow. Every barn, cottage gable and solitary tree stood out in sharp silhouette, delineated in perfect detail in the clear evening light.

Inevitably such perfection was short lived. The beauty of the western heavens faded as quickly as it had appeared, as the yelps of little owls heralded the approach of nightfall. Soon only the twinkle of a faraway light served as a reminder of the distant sweep of the wolds and it was time to turn for home.

The clustered white heads of yarrow flowers stood out like dim beacons by the wayside as I descended the hill into the village. A bat quartered noiselessly under a street lamp in search of the moths that find such islands of light irresistible.

13 September 1980

ALMOST twenty years have passed since the last train travelled the old branch line and over ten since I last walked this length of track.

Then, even though the wooden sleepers had only recently been removed, nature had already commenced the inevitable process of reclamation. Tufts of spiky grass protruded from the ballast and spindly stems of ragwort, hawkweed and willow herb rose from the inhospitable surface to colonise the ground and slowly, imperceptibly, return the so-called permanent way to its one-time wild state.

The first of the woody plants, the sallows, had also begun to encroach from the adjacent embankment, and a discerning eye could detect the forerunners of the invasion of hawthorns — mere wispy spikes as yet — but a start had been made. The process was under way.

And now, a decade later, and without any interference from man apart from the steps of an occasional passer-by, the cycle of natural regeneration has been firmly established and is gathering momentum with each succeeding season. The ballast layer has disappeared completely, overlaid by a mat of dense ground vegetation. The trailblazing hawthorns and sallows, sturdy thriving bushes by now, have been joined by a sprawling jungle of other woody species — ash, Turkey oak, sycamore, blackthorn, elder, buckthorn, and many more.

Each of these newcomers is a mere cog in the wheel of the regenerative cycle which will in time culminate in the return of deciduous woodland — the natural ground cover before our ancestors embarked on the clearance of the mighty forests in prehistoric times.

This of course pre-supposes that man will not interfere once more to frustrate nature's schemes — a rash assumption. In the meantime however, the process continues, and the last traces of a Victorian 'permanent way' disappear into oblivion.

14 November 1981

JUDGING by its size and the gnarled and contorted state of its mighty boughs, the blackened oak has borne witness to well over three centuries of change.

It spreads its great canopy over the bridleway which descends from the village to the old water mill, where corn was ground from Norman times until the early years of the present century. The rate of change, which has accelerated steadily within living memory, has culminated in the transformation of the mill itself. The semi-derelict building has been thoroughly modernised and the mill pond and leat restored after years of neglect. Needless to say, this restoration has been effected not to bring about the return of corn-grinding, but to create a country residence, and the setting could hardly be bettered.

For the mill stands by the delightful little River Dikler, which picks its tortuous and unobtrusive way through lush meadows on its course to join the Windrush, scarcely a country mile distant.

Eyebrows — and voices too — were raised a couple of years ago when the mill's new owners sought permission to divert the ancient right-of-way which passed the mill-house door to cross the leat by the long-still wheel. Time has worked its healing ways since then however, and now the walker takes a gentle diversion beyond the old oak, to cross the mill stream by a pleasant little footbridge and rejoin the original track a few strides beyond the mill.

It is two fields distant where the greatest change of recent times has taken place. It was but yesterday, in terms of the old oak's life span, that the ground was torn away in the search for gravel. And yet, ten years after the excavation ceased the scars have healed and the veteran oak looks down on the miniature lakeland, where coots call and mallard come winging in at dusk.

20 February 1982

50

Wold Landscape

WHAT better place could there be to spend a summer afternoon than on one of the surviving stretches of Cotswold downland, spared, on account of its steepness, from the despoiling blade of the plough?

What at first glance appears to be a somewhat unremarkable and bare hillside reveals itself on closer inspection to consist of an incredibly rich and diverse community of plants and animals, living out their lives in an unimproved-grassland habitat now all too rare in our intensely-cultivated countryside.

I use the term closer inspection deliberately, for unless we are prepared to linger and look, forgetting the pressures of time and other commitments, we can gain but a vague and superficial idea of the intricate web of life around us.

Summer lime-loving flowers spangle the short turf in abundance. Some, such as wild thyme, eyebright, trefoil and squinancywort, cover the turf. Others — rock rose, dropwort, scabious, knapweed and bellflower — add their share of colour at a level above the carpet of ground cover. Such a variety of flowering plants ensures a wealth of insect life. The air is alive with the buzz of bees and the rasping of grasshoppers, while a host of smaller insects scurry to and fro among the foliage.

Butterflies abound. The elegant marbled white is in its element in these conditions, vying in numbers with the ubiquitous meadow browns, which flutter lazily by in the heat. Both large and small skippers are everywhere plentiful, often basking with their wings held in that distinctive moth-like manner peculiar to their kind, or whirring from flower to flower with single-minded purpose.

Downland bird life in July is predictably limited. Yellowhammers wheeze out their monotonous notes from the edge of the nearby scrub and a turtle dove's purring song sets the seal on this limestone downland summer scene.

24 July 1982

ON THE flank of the slope above the village, where the road sweeps in a steep curve before making its final abrupt ascent to the ridge from the valley below, the discerning walker can find a fragment of the old Cotswold landscape that is fast disappearing in these changing modern times.

In effect little more than a stretch of extended roadside verge, this crescent-shaped fragment of uneven waste ground supports a population of plant and animal life apparently out of proportion to its modest size.

At first glance there appears little cause to linger here. The road carries a fair amount of traffic, with its attendant noise and unwholesome smell. The old hedgerow climbing the slope from the last houses of the village for some reason peters out nearby, and is replaced by a somewhat stark wooden fence. Uncultivated and for the most part untended by the roadman's blade, the piece of ground is nonetheless impinged upon by human pressures throughout the year. Picnicking families occasionally spread themselves over its less-inhospitable areas during the summer. Litter is constantly strewn along its outer margin. In winter it is regularly trampled by horses and used as a parking lot for horseboxes when the hunt meets nearby.

After heavy rain the ground becomes a quagmire pocked with treacherous ruts. In times of drought these indentations are turned rock hard and are thus equally difficult to negotiate. Yet despite these varied and largely adverse influences, this tiny corner of unclaimed land abounds in riches. The sprinkling of coltsfoot, lesser celandine, cowslip and lady's smock of spring is succeeded by a host of delightful summer flowers, to which clouds of butterflies are irresistibly drawn.

No doubt many such corners of wild Cotswold exist and their presence gives pleasure to people who, like me, never tire of watching wild life of the commonplace kind wherever it can be found. It would be a sad day if efficiency and tidy-mindedness combined to deprive us of such untamed corners as these.

24 September 1983

52

I APPROACHED the site of the lost village along a muddy footpath from its nearest neighbour. Although this entailed scarcely a mile of walking, it was a relief to drop into the lane and to be able to scrape away some of the mud that had weighed down my boots and reduced my stride to a stagger.

As my map indicated, only two groups of farm buildings had survived to bear witness to the fact that there had once been a village here, and to perpetuate its name. They stood, some half a mile apart, at the extremities of the settlement. Both were substantial buildings, obviously old, though whether their origins were traceable to the time when there had been a village here it was impossible to say.

Certainly the barn associated with one of these farms bore the stamp of the best in Cotswold vernacular architecture. Built like a church, with the fine proportions and attention to detail comparable with some of the better known barns, it must surely have seen the decline and final disappearance of the village that once stood in the adjoining field.

For disappeared the place undoubtedly had. All that remained were a series of ridges, hollows and associated low mounds scattered over the field. According to my map, the village had been arranged in some kind of pattern, possibly with streets separating the houses, but at ground level, even with the vegetation in its winter state, this was difficult to appreciate.

Why had this village withered and died, while its neighbour, barely a mile distant, had survived and flourished? Had the dreaded plague struck here, causing the place to be deserted and allowed to crumble away? Or was sheep enclosure responsible, as in the case of so many Cotswold villages? Or could it be that some tyrannical landlord, exercising the absolute power that all too often led to absolute corruption, had for some selfish reason had the place swept away on a mere whim? Hardly likely perhaps, yet such actions were not unknown in our rural past.

If every field can be likened to a page of unwritten history, a whole volume lies beneath those humps and hollows.

21 January 1984

THE ODD half-hour snatched from the day's demands, and spent in some hidden corner of the Cotswolds, can sometimes prove to be as refreshing and memorable as a day's carefully planned ramble.

Thankfully pulling off the main road, along which the subtle beauty of the landscape had been reduced to a detached and distorted blur of fleeting impressions, I found myself once more in a world of permanence and quiet harmony, unchanged from the days when I first discovered it, twenty or so years before.

Leaving the car on the edge of the village, I was soon happily remote from the seething workaday world, exchanging the hard, uncompromising road for a deserted lane, alongside which fine beeches towered, hemmed in by budding hedges with glimpses of rolling fields fading into a wood-fringed distance.

Away in the hollow beyond the beeches, the first marsh marigolds of the year revealed their opulent beauty in the April sunshine. An array of lesser celandines carpeted the nearby turf, while beneath the ashes, a cloud of ice-blue wood anemones swayed like a mirage in the gentlest of breezes.

My destination — if it could be called such on this all-too-brief diversion from duty — was the old church among the trees, left behind yet never finally abandoned when the village moved up the hill centuries ago. Here, flowers are still placed on graves scattered among ancient lichen-encrusted tombstones. The only sounds to assail the ears are the clamour of rooks in the crowns of the beeches and the wheezing and chattering of the starlings engaged in their courtship rituals amid the pockmarked lower boughs.

Nearby, bordering the bridleway, I lingered to admire once more the fluted trunks of the hornbeams before turning — renewed yet reluctant — and retracing my steps to rejoin the mainstream of modern life.

28 April 1984

54

Wold Landscape

THE RIDGE and furrow of the ancient ploughing pattern was accentuated by the retreating snow as I followed a field path on the edge of the wolds recently.

The curved parallel lines of the old furrows stood out like white ribs on a green-ridged backcloth — evidence that the old pasture was once arable, at a time when ox ploughs were an everyday sight across the Cotswolds. Except when the wolds lie under snow, the best time to observe old cultivation patterns is on a sunny evening, when the contrasting bands of light and shadow reveal a great deal of how the fields were once used.

I have been studying a photograph of an ox-plough team, taken in the Cotswolds early in the present century. The six oxen are yoked in pairs, led by a boy, with the ploughman steering the heavy plough along some dozen yards or so behind the heads of the leading beasts. It was the sheer bulk and unwieldiness of these teams, which often comprised four pairs of oxen on heavy soils, that gave rise to the reversed 'S' pattern so often associated with old ploughland, and revealed so strikingly in aerial photographs.

In order to avoid the team trampling on the adjacent strips and ridges, the ploughman began his task by assembling his team on the narrow headland at right angles to the line he intended to follow, thus avoiding damage to nearby crops and creating a parallel headland at the opposite end of the field.

It presents something of a challenge to try to deduce what local variations on this general pattern applied to a particular area. The answer lies — if not exactly in the soil — then at least under the grass beneath our feet.

19 January 1985

THE SOUTHERN slopes of Bredon Hill abound with springs.

The tiny streams arising from these water issues have cut their miniature valleys steeply into Bredon's flank, each groove contributing to the overall weathered and time-wrinkled appearance of the hill's southward face.

Yet as the ravages of time bestow character upon the human countenance, so Bredon's distinction owes much to the ceaseless erosive power of these swift-flowing streams.

Long fingers of woodland reach their way up the tapering cleft of each valley, while further downstream, venerable old trees, a network of mixed hedgerows and a scatter of orchards combine to add diversity to the scene.

Lower still, these gushing streams provided ideal sites for the ancient settlements from which grew the chain of villages now flourishing on Bredon Hill. These well-loved names — Kemerton, Overbury, Conderton, Grafton, Ashton-under-Hill, Elmley Castle — all bear testimony to the life-giving water which had descended from Bredon's slopes to swell first the Carrant Brook and later the rivers Avon and Severn long before early man first settled here.

My Christmastide ramble over Bredon concluded with a descent along one of these tiny valleys. Recent rainwater gushed from land-drain and culvert, swelling the current of the nameless stream. A grey wagtail picked its dainty way among the mossy boulders near where the torrent poured itself along an ivy-fringed channel hemmed in by trees. A glance at my map showed that early man had chosen the upper reaches of this little valley for his settlement long before the village nestling below had come into being. These primitive people had laboured to build a fort above the spring, thus ensuring a reliable water supply, for even in the driest of summers, this trickle never ceases completely.

Reaching the village I lost sight of the stream as it skirted farms and gardens on its descent. The map-makers had encountered a similar problem, I discovered — the thin blue line on my map came to an abrupt stop — only to reappear half a mile or so downstream.

4 January 1986

56

EVERY Cotswold village had its quarry — or quarr, as it was known in local speech.

Tracing the precise location of these features can be a time consuming and frustrating exercise for many old quarries have not been worked for many years and have been more or less reclaimed by nature. Larger, more recent quarries frequently disappear from view entirely, filled up with rubbish — a sad and ignominious end for an industrial relic which yielded the stone from which some of the finest buildings in the country were fashioned.

The sites of some of the most celebrated Cotswold quarries lie along the Windrush valley, spanning the Gloucestershire-Oxfordshire border, and on a sparkling winter's day I set out to find what traces I could of some of these ancient sources of the best in Cotswold stone.

My search began just over the border — at the little village of Taynton, close to Burford. Although long since closed, I discovered that a small quantity of this superb limestone is still quarried to satisfy local needs. My walk along the bridleway leading towards the Stow-Burford road took me by the substantial remains of the quarries from which the stone used by Christopher Wren for the rebuilding of St. Paul's Cathedral was obtained. Many of the Oxford colleges too, owe their being to this stone, which was also used in the building of St. George's Chapel at Windsor.

Such was the reputation of Taynton stone that it was carried by road across the upper Thames valley as far as Radcot Bridge, where it was loaded on to boats and shipped to London. The results of the masons' handiwork is admired by countless visitors, while the quarries from which the precious stone was obtained lie deserted and, except by a few, forgotten.

25 January 1986

TO THE physical geographer, the dip in the scarp near the headwaters of the rivers Isbourne and Windrush is an air or water gap, so called because the rivers at some point in geological time combined to threaten to breach the scarp at this point.

However, I suspect that most passing walkers, like myself, are content merely to stop and admire the view. For the combe opens out northwards to reveal a stretch of superb scenery, with woods clinging to the valley sides and a chequerwork of fields fading away into the distance.

Early farmers left their mark here too. Evidence of their strip lynchets can be seen clearly on the upper slopes — a reminder that this corner of high Cotswold has been cultivated for centuries.

A farm and a tiny cluster of cottages stand near the dip at the junction of two lanes. Beyond the last barn, an old green lane, reduced now in width to a mere footpath, climbs the slope by the side of a wood on its long journey southwards. A public bridleway sign has been erected here recently but I fancy that few riders come this way.

Although metalled, the lane following the southward-flowing stream is signposted as unsuitable for motors and consequently the walker can enjoy comparative peace along its narrow sinuous way. The stream gurgles unconcernedly along its hidden course, its banks bedecked with willow herb, cranesbill, self-heal, and a host of other moisture-seeking flowers throughout spring and summer.

Beyond two narrow ponds, where the stream has been dammed in recent times, the little valley opens out and a considerable tract of woodland looms ahead. A solitary cottage nestles beneath the first of the trees, framed in a setting as near to perfection as I for one, can contemplate. Soon, both lane and stream are swallowed up in dense woodland, through which they pick their way for close on a mile before emerging out on to open wold.

Here the stream, like the lane, meets another and a secret corner of the Cotswolds is left behind.

16 August 1986

By Lane & Footpath

THE BRIDLEWAY linking our village with its neighbour over the wold strikes off across the fields only a short distance from my cottage.

Its rough surface, dusty in summer, has been churned into a sea of mud by passing cattle since the recent heavy rains and the walker without gumboots needs to pick his way with great care to avoid the unexpected pot-holes and treacherous flooded ruts.

After passing the village allotments, the bridleway dips between straggly hedges, from which several gnarled and knobbly ash trees sprout at intervals, their ancient trunks bound tightly by clasping cords of ivy. Close by stands a rickety five-barred gate, secured to its post by the inevitable binder twine. Just off the track once stood a fine cluster of elms. A dozen or so rooks' nests tossed in the handsome crowns, visible for some distance, but now alas they are no more — gone like the tall trees — and the birds have been forced to search elsewhere for nesting sites.

Mutilated stumps can still be seen protruding from a bed of rank nettles and a great cone of ash denotes the spot where the diseased trunks were consigned to the flames. But at least these fine trees were spared the indignity of others in the next village — left to stand in peeled lifeless witness to the ravages of Dutch elm disease.

The character of the bridleway changes beyond the gate. An old unkempt hedge bounds it on one side, its hawthorn, blackthorn, crab apple and bramble forming an impenetrable barrier. A single wild cherry adds a touch of grace to the scene, while away to the left, beyond the fence, two furrowed pastures climb towards the horizon, formed by a dense wood from which pheasants call.

A comparatively recent planting of poplars adds a certain novelty further along the bridleway. All trace of the village has disappeared by now and soon the first distant view of the next village appears through leafless trees, the houses clinging to the slopes in true Cotswold fashion.

17 November 1979

FEW WALKERS trod the footpath through the old hazel coppice when I first knew it.

Uncut and unrestricted, the hazels thrust their outer branches across the narrow path from either side, while the upper growth formed a leafy tunnel through which the sun's rays cast a dappled shadow on the flowery sward.

All has changed now, however. Since the footpath became part of the Oxfordshire Way long distance footpath, its delights have been revealed to a wider public. Throughout the year, groups of ramblers traverse its length, ensuring that the ancient right-of-way will not be allowed to fall into disuse, as have many paths in the locality.

Prolonged and regular use exerts its price of course, and although the problem is in no way comparable with that causing so much concern in some of our national parks, the cost is considerable. Low-lying stretches of the way are reduced to a quagmire after heavy rain, causing walkers to divert from the main path and thus trampling the marginal ground flora. Litter too, begins to obtrude, even though the majority of those using the path comply faithfully with the country code.

A wide diversity of flowering plants is associated with hazel coppice woodland and this tract is no exception. April sees the rich green spikes of bluebell leaves mingling with those of the wild arum, giving promise of a haze of blue a few weeks hence. By contrast, the delicate grace of the wood sorrel foliage is of a distinctive pale green. This plant will contribute its own share of floral colour soon as its small, white blooms unfurl beneath the hazels.

A few old oaks tower above the hazels at intervals. Their inconspicuous flowers were just emerging as I looked up from the hazel tassels into a cloudless spring sky.

16 April 1983

FROM ITS junction with the modern road, the old lane plunges under the beeches and strikes off boldly across the open wold.

Little more than a flattened ditch, flanked by a low bank on one side and the vestiges of an old wall interspersed with blackthorn thicket on the other, it affords the walker an alluring glimpse of a gently rolling expanse of upland landscape.

Away to the right, a sweep of mixed woodland provides a multicoloured backdrop. At one time though, trees played a far greater part in the structure of this corner of the Cotswolds than they do now. The carpet of dog's mercury underfoot is a sure indicator of this and it is tempting to imagine the old lane advancing beneath the shade of giant forest trees, unknown except to the passing cattle-drover or woodcutter.

Sheepwalks replaced the cleared woodland but now they too, have gone. The enclosed fields that succeeded them have long been broken by the plough and support little wild life, apart from the occasional skylark, one of which rose in full-throated song as I passed.

Beyond the derelict cottage — the only habitation along the route for a mile or more on either side — the course of the old lane was until recently lost in a tangle of thorn and briar. Now however, the lane is being opened up once more and soon it will be possible to follow its gentle descent between the hazel-lined banks, where mossy roots intertwine and primroses beautify the dark earth before the green mantle spreads to cover the bare ground.

I look forward to coming this way again as the year advances and this long-lost stretch of the old lane basks under summer skies.

20 April 1985

By Lane and Footpath

'EXCUSE ME, but are you looking for a footpath?'

I had followed the clearly-signposted track for over a mile to reach the road but contrary to my map, there was no evidence of the right-of-way continuing over the next field.

The man wound down his car window and we compared notes on the frustrations of following footpaths. He had lived in the area for over 40 years, I learned, and during that time had witnessed the loss of many of the old paths he had known as a young man. Together with his brother, he had made a point of walking as many of the paths as he could to prevent them from falling into disuse but this was no longer possible with the passing of the years.

The disappearance of this particular path was a matter of keen regret to him. He recalled countless happy wanderings along its course and commiserated with me in being denied the experience. He went on to say that it had been ploughed up and fenced off about six years since — the work of the prominent landowning family to whom most of the surrounding countryside belonged. Their power was virtually unchallengeable, he asserted. He knew for a fact that the uprooted footpath sign lay in a corner of the estate-office yard to this day and that there was no intention of restoring it to its rightful place.

My informant bid me good day and drove off, leaving me in something of a dilemma. I could of course, press on over the vast featureless arable field, in the hope of finding my route as shown on my map. This did not seem a particularly pleasant prospect however, so I opted with some reluctance to return to my starting point partly by road, with the intention of picking up another footpath to complete my walk.

But even this alternative was not without annoyance. One gate along the route was locked and a stile was missing further on. What should have been a pleasant, relaxing walk was spoilt by what may charitably be called insensitivity, or more accurately arrogance, on the part of a landowner.

17 May 1986

CAMPDEN LANE is the name by which the old track is known, according to the map. The name Campden refers to the town, a fair distance away northwards from here, but with the creation of the Cotswold Way long-distance footpath, part of the lane at least serves in something like its former function.

But it is the lower, lesser-known section of the lane that I like best. From its junction with the quiet road to Farmcote, it plunges between deep hedges as though anxious to exchange the open country for a secret world of its own making.

Soon, after a steady climb, the last fleeting glimpses of the distant Malverns, of Bredon Hill, and of its associated scattered outliers, are left behind, excluded by a virtual tunnel of thorn and scrambling briar, hazel and wayfaring tree, woodbine and ivy.

Beyond the old quarry, where a crumbling field wall is supported by the tangle of ivy that once hastened its ruin, the lane opens out, surfacing once more to admit the sunlight, which transforms the shady sward into a miniature meadow. Here, rabbits burrow in the open air, a few birches thrive without competition from rival trees, and early butterflies bask when the sun puts in a belated appearance.

The next phase of its progress sees the lane flanked by dark and mysterious blackthorn thickets, beneath which little else can flourish except a spiky carpet of dog's mercury, a relic of the time when thick woodland covered much of this high wold country. The remains of a stone wall are scarcely visible beneath this impenetrable barrier, where chaffinches sing lustily and yellowhammers wheeze their monotonous refrain.

From the gaps between these overgrown stretches, the walker along Campden Lane catches glimpses of the wide wold landscape rising and falling on either side. The eye is drawn to distant farms tucked snugly into gentle hollows and crowns of woodland rise above the growing corn.

Beyond a belt of conifers, alien in this landscape, the old lane sweeps on to be met by the Cotswold Way climbing up from Hailes Abbey by way of Beckbury Camp, with Stumps Cross but a short stride away on the summit of Stanway Hill.

24 May 1986

THE UNSUSPECTING walker descending the sunken lane from the road to the old mill pond is in for something of a surprise.

The lane leaves the busy road and dips beneath a holly hedge, with views of the little valley fringed on its far bank by a belt of woodland, stretching eastwards. Later in the year this view will be restricted somewhat as the foliage of the nearby trees spreads a canopy overhead. Meanwhile the plants colonising the open bank make the most of the spring sunshine. Wild arum puts up its vivid green leaves, lesser celandines cover the bare soil, and dog's mercury pushes through the hedge as though the woodland of former times still clothed these Cotswold slopes.

It is when the walker reaches the foot of the slope, where the footpath up the valley emerges over a stile by the woodland edge, that the impact of recent change strikes.

Gone is the wild and weed-choked expanse of water that I, like many a passing walker, delighted to linger by. Gone too, is the clutter of trees and bushes that always promised — without ever actually producing — a surprising bird or two from within its tangled sprawl.

Instead, a new clean symmetrical pond, complete with dam, lies alongside the little river, gurgling beneath its trees. Vast quantities of earth have been removed, the site levelled, and new trees planted to soften the harshness of the scene.

This healing process will take time, however. How long, one wonders, will it be before the kingcups return in their golden glory and a hint of hidden promise touches the imagination as before?

Two hopeful signs appeared before I moved on, prompting me to take an optimistic view of the future of this little corner of the Cotswolds. The first was the harsh squawk of an unseen moorhen which though banished from its reedy haunts, remained nearby on the river.

The second was the sight of a slow worm, basking beneath the hedge, and which allowed me to study its bronze motionless form without stirring as late-March sunshine warmed the ground.

4 April 1987

'NO PUBLIC way here', proclaims the moss-capped stone in the woods.

Resembling an old milestone of the kind still to be seen along some of our Cotswold roads, it stands by the bridleway as a reminder to travellers that the track curving away under the trees from the right-of-way is a private path. Overgrown and scarcely discernible, it was once the exclusive domain of the local landowner. Now however, the woods are the property of a forestry company and the carefully-incised notice is passed by unheeded, except perhaps by those walkers who, new to these parts and unfamiliar with the route, are grateful for the message it imparts.

Not all notices of this kind are similarly helpful, or for that matter couched in such inoffensive terms. We are all familiar with the 'Keep out' and 'Trespassers will be prosecuted' signs which plaster trees, gates and buildings and obtrude in the countryside. No doubt the perpetrators of this vandalism would argue that having been troubled by thoughtless, even malicious intruders on their land, such a drastic response is justified. But surely the jarring effect of these eyesores can only be regretted.

There is of course a lighter side to the warning-sign issue. I once came across a laboriously-handpainted notice on which the signwriter, having grappled successfully with the spelling of 'trespassers' and 'prosecuted', had blotted his copybook by inserting 'definately' in an unfortunate attempt to add extra impact.

Another landowner hit upon the idea of exploiting fear as a weapon with which to deter trespass, and came up with 'Beware adders. If bitten, get in touch with a doctor without delay'.

'Beware of the bull', an old favourite, is not so common with recent changes in the law but it would be stretching sentiment to the limit to lament its passing.

The intentionally-humorous sign is a comparatively recent phenomenon by comparison. A notable example, to be seen at Bledington, near Stow-on-the-Wold, a village justly proud of its stream-fringed green and associated bird life, warns motorists — and not without reason — 'Slow. Ducks crossing'.

5 December 1987

By Lane and Footpath

EVERY COTSWOLD country lane has its own distinctive character but Mill Lane possesses a combination of qualities that make it unique.

Its name is something of a mystery. There is no trace of a mill anywhere in the vicinity, in fact no building of any kind can be seen along its entire length. Like so many pleasant country lanes, it owes a good deal of its charm to the fact that it leads to nowhere in particular and is therefore little frequented by the traffic that has reduced so many lanes to mere thoroughfares.

Another of Mill Lane's appealing features is its sunken state. Like many Devon and Somerset lanes, it winds its tortuous way beneath banks topped by ancient hedges, the canopies of which meet overhead to create a tunnel-like effect, seen at its best when sunlight dapples the vegetation or at night by car headlights.

Although its steep-sided banks may appear at first glance to be less botanically rich than the grassy verges along so many of our lanes, this impression is not borne out by investigation.

By late February, the first yellow stars of the lesser celandine are beginning to appear, with wild violets not far behind. May sees greater stitchwort's dainty white blooms emerge to gladden the eye, with a host of familiar summer flowers ensuring a colourful succession as the year advances.

As befits old hedges, a wide variety of woody plants can be seen along the lane. The earliest to flower is cherry plum, whose pure white flowers on large loose spikes appear before those of its relative the blackthorn. These were in evidence by mid-February, spangling the upper reaches of the lane, not far from the hollow remnant of an old oak, which loses a little more of its decaying timber whenever a severe wind sweeps down the lane.

Generations of local people have travelled Mill lane — for business or pleasure — over the centuries. Horse riders enjoy their passage beneath the leafy canopy and occasionally a group of ramblers or cyclists discover its delights. At dusk, as human activity decreases, the animals take over. A foraging badger ambles through the shadows and wary foxes skulk beneath the woody tangle.

27 February 1988

A Cotswold Country Diary

FROM THE little hamlet, perched on the flank of the ridge, the track winds its way down to the abbey ruins, nestling beneath the trees in the valley below.

Unlike the ancient Salt Way, which strikes off over the slopes in a roughly parallel course westwards, the track has been spared the dull conformity resulting from being classified as a road. Instead, it retains its bridleway status, has a stony uneven surface rather than a smooth tarmac one, and is a walker's delight.

Woodland hems it in on the right. This is primary woodland, rare alas in these parts nowadays, older by far than the old track, or for that matter, than the 13th century abbey. Small-leaved lime is the predominant tree, and has been coppiced since man first discovered the advantages of this woodland craft in these parts, long, long, ago.

In April the woodland fringe is a riot of wild flowers. Violets tinge the once-barren turf and clumps of primroses splash delicate colour beneath bare trunks. As well as limes, old oaks tower above the hazel and field-maple understorey. Many of these veterans are well past their prime, and signs of die-back are clearly evident. They serve as hosts to countless small creatures — woodpeckers, tits, moths, beetles — and their fallen relatives are exploited by other creatures as decay accelerates.

And now, after six months' absence, this ancient wood echoes with one of the most gladdening sounds of spring. 'Chiff-chaff, chiff-chaff', calls the tiny olive-coloured warbler as it searches for small insects in the uppermost branches. I suspect that it has been back for several days, possibly before March expired, for its refrain is vigorous and prolonged.

By the woodland edge, another lime-loving shrub is stirring into life. This is the wayfaring tree, aptly named in this setting. Its flat umbels are already beginning to emerge alongside its wrinkled oval leaves.

It is with reluctance that I leave this stony woodside track and passing the abbey ruins, step on to a smooth sleek road where walking, though easy, loses much of its delight.

16 April 1988

68

Along the Waterside

AFTER SHAKING off the confines of Bourton-on-the-Water, the Windrush becomes an untrammelled secret river once more.

Picking its way through a gentle landscape, it gurgles softly to itself in reedy pools, hurries over pebbly shallows and plunges through clumps of willows, as though thankful to make good its escape from the self-styled 'Venice of the Cotswolds'.

By the time it receives its delightful little tributary, the Dikler, below the Rissingtons, it has completely regained its quiet evasive character and emerges into open country almost unscathed, except for the inevitable scraps of flotsam carried down from the tourist-trap upstream.

This phase of the river's life is known only to a few patient anglers and discriminating walkers. I had the riverside footpath to myself on a mild mid-October afternoon recently, and paused to watch the blotched and stippled leaves drifting steadily down, many falling into the rusty blades of the reeds lining the waterside, others, especially the feather-like leaves of the willows, breaking their fall on the water itself, and being carried along like a flotilla of miniature boats, by the swiftly-moving current.

A few late flowers added a touch of bolder colour to the scene. Forget-me-nots were still in full bloom by the muddy margins and the last of the water figwort flowers were putting on their modest show. Comfrey also contributed its share of brightness along the bank and late dandelions, gaudy as ever, were not to be outdone.

Moles had been active recently on the river bank and a heap of fox droppings on one of the hills, together with signs of scratching and scattered soil, suggested that the predator had worked hard to obtain a meal of mole, though whether or not it had been successful it was impossible to tell.

A cry of alarm and clatter of wings shattered the silence as a moorhen trod the water from almost under my feet, reminding me that I was an intruder in this little-frequented stretch of the Windrush Valley, where wild things live out their lives undisturbed.

27 October 1979

THE CHAIN of flooded gravel pits in the valley below the village provide a type of habitat somewhat unusual in the Cotswolds.

Although man-made, created within the last decade, they have become a permanent and accepted feature of the local landscape and being easily accessible along a network of public footpaths, they provide a welcome opportunity to observe the behaviour of a range of waterfowl throughout the year.

The resident population consists of moorhen, coot, mute swan, great-crested grebe, little grebe, mallard and tufted duck. Herons appear regularly and kingfishers are frequent visitors. During the winter months, the waterfowl population is augmented by the arrival of flocks of pochard — handsome diving ducks which add a touch of novelty to the scene and on a recent visit I spent some time getting familiar with this welcome addition to our local bird life.

Drake pochards have dark chestnut heads, black breasts and grey bodies, while the females are brownish on the head and breast with a characteristic yellowish facial band. Both sexes have an unmistakable pale blue stripe on the bill which can be seen at a considerable distance.

I had chosen a mild, still December afternoon for my visit and about fifty pochard sat motionless in the watery sunshine, their heads either sunk on their breasts or buried in the plumage of their closed wings. Nearby, a flotilla of mallard paddled across the pit, the velvet green of the drakes' necks prominently displayed. Coots dotted the water, feeding and quarrelling noisily from time to time, and a solitary great-crested grebe stretched out its graceful neck by the low squat island in mid-water.

The short afternoon was well advanced by now and I set off back towards the village. Suddenly a rhythmic splashing and beating of wings sounded from over the hedge and a pair of swans rose into view and made off into a golden sunset.

15 December 1979

A Cotswold Country Diary

AS THOUGH to compensate for its total absence on the previous day, when grey brooding skies threatened to bring more rain, the sun shone virtually without interruption, uplifting the spirits, enriching the songs of the birds, and prompting the midges to dance as though on invisible puppet strings in the warm air.

By the riverside, signs of new emerging life abounded everywhere. Freshly unfurled leaves of great willow-herb, iris, teasel, dock, comfrey and dead nettle protruded from the mat of dead vegetation and waterborne debris deposited when the water level fell following the winter rains. Soon this new growth will cover the banks with lushness. Last year's dead stems will disappear and the river will become a thing of hidden delights as burgeoning growth forms an impenetrable tunnel of dense aromatic vegetation.

In the meantime it is comparatively easy to follow the river's tortuous course. It weaves its way between ancient split and contorted willows, the tips of whose drooping branches skim the rushing water. Some of these branches bear the telltale evidence of debris carried on the winter flood, when the little river, swollen to overflowing, flowed cloudy and deep, its waters lapping the bank, its character transformed from a secret stream to a surging torrent.

Now, back to its normal state, the river's shallows are too inviting to resist. While wading along one such stretch, I was able to see familiar features from unfamiliar perspectives — always a novel experience. It was while proceeding in this way that the distinctive call of an approaching bird caused me to stop and wait expectantly. Within seconds, round a bend in the river ahead, a dipper sped into view, its white bib-patch prominent as it neared me on rapidly beating wings. It passed within feet of my still form before disappearing from sight round the next bend upstream.

15 March 1980

THE WIT who described early rising as a triumph of mind over mattress certainly had a point — it requires a certain amount of willpower to drag oneself from a comfortable bed at daybreak. Once made however, the effort is well worthwhile, as I discovered on a fine mild morning in early August.

Every woodpigeon for miles around seemed to be cooing its dawn greeting as I descended the field path into the valley, where the dim outlines of distant treetops seemed to hang in mid-air above the blanket of mist.

Overhead, a sudden thud of air prompted me to look up. A closely-packed flock of lapwings were moving rapidly across the morning sky, following the river's snaking course. I crossed the rickety footbridge and soon reached the first of the flooded gravel pits but my cautious approach did not deceive the heron, which rose on heavy wings and made off into the mist.

Tall stout stems of reed mace bristled by the water's edge, where an agitated sedge warbler wove its way between the leaf blades, scolding me with a babble of stuttering wheezing notes. The dark forms of coots moved off to the security of deeper water, leaving V-shaped ripples on the glassy surface, while in the distance, shrouded in the enveloping mist, a pair of mute swans regarded me warily.

Further along the bank, clumps of water mint were coming into bloom and I bent to pinch a leaf to enjoy the tangy aroma. A fine stand of great willow-herb — codlins and cream to country people in the days when local names, always colourful and more often than not remarkably apt, were fashionable — was bursting into flower nearby. Its welcome pink glow provided a foretaste of the colours soon to be revealed as sunshine finally banished the departing mist.

9 August 1980

A Cotswold Country Diary

OF THE scores of visitors thronging the banks of the River Coln at Bibury, how many take the trouble to discover something of its delights further upstream?

The 'Clear Coln', as the poet called it, offers a unique blend of beauty and historical association. The Romans knew it well. Between its source — on the flanks of Cleeve Common — and Fossebridge, the fording place for their highway to Corinium, they built a chain of settlements, the most famous of which is Chedworth Villa.

Some fifteen centuries later, the valley of the Coln was again invaded — this time by railway engineers, who constructed their line in a series of sweeping curves to connect Cheltenham with Cirencester. Today, the ancient Fosse Way is the bustling A429, and few of those travelling it trouble to seek out the little river, gurgling unobtrusively in its steep valley below. The railway has gone, of course, and there is little to disturb the calm as the Coln flows on through a gentle pastoral landscape before emerging to help create the widely-acclaimed charm of Bibury.

My own favourite stretch of the Coln lies between the villages of Coln St. Dennis and Coln Rogers. Here is a plantsman's paradise, where ancient willows and alders fringe the river bank and the way is gladdened by great clumps of water dock, willow herb, meadowsweet and hemp agrimony. Strands of emerald river crowfoot stretch for yards in the swift current, studding the water with white blossoms, while at intervals gaudy monkey flowers add rich contrast, aided and abetted by patches of starry-flowered stonecrop covering the low grey field walls.

A mallard duck shepherding her flotilla of ducklings were my sole companions as I followed the Coln from tiny Calcot down to Coln Rogers recently. Approaching the village all was quiet apart from the screams of the swifts, skimming round the church tower in the late-afternoon sky.

18 July 1981

THE OLD gated footbridge has gone. The last crossing-place over the River Dikler before it offers up its waters to the larger Windrush has at last been replaced by a new safe solid structure which should serve the walker well for years to come.

Those of us who have tramped the footpath regularly over the years had learned to negotiate the old bridge and had grown accustomed to its alarmingly dilapidated state. After avoiding the clump of virulent nettles sprouting by the rickety gatepost on each bank, we had gingerly picked our way across its tilted uneven surface, while at the same time resisting the temptation to grip the one surviving handrail, which wobbled violently under the least pressure, as though threatening to join its long-departed fellow in the swirling water below.

The pastime of gazing contemplatively from bridges is an old one, as old surely as bridges themselves. Who can resist taking the view from the parapet of an ancient bridge — or a new one for that matter. The view from a bridge gives us a refreshingly new perspective from that afforded by either bank. It constitutes one of the minor pleasures of exploring the countryside.

The old footbridge was no exception. From its rickety frame I have accumulated a handful of treasured experiences over the years — a pair of swans drifting regally downstream; a metallic-tinted dragonfly hovering over the water; the lazy splash of a trout breaking the stillness of a summer evening; the glimpse of pure gold as the first iris opened by the waterside.

Now, resting my elbows on the firm handrail, I anticipate fresh delights as I linger on the new bridge at this old crossing-place.

26 September 1981

WHATEVER the time of year, a walk in the vicinity of the meeting place of our two local rivers never fails to produce an abundant variety of wild life.

The moment we leave the road behind and set off along the footpath by the hedge side, every stride is one of expectancy. For the hedge itself is an ancient one, rich in different species of trees and shrubs and even in November there is much to notice and enjoy.

The maples in particular delight the eye with their range of gold, bronze and fiery red, followed closely by the hawthorns, multicoloured too, though in a more subdued fashion. The hazel and blackthorn offer a less ostentatious blend of buff and yellow while the oaks, ashes and sycamores aspire merely to a blotched mixture of brown and faded green.

Unlike any of these, the solitary buckthorn along the hedge still retains its summer green, which together with its clusters of shiny black berries makes a striking contrast with the mellow tints on either side.

Myriads of midges dance in the calm air by the footbridge, where the rusty blades of withered reeds tremble slightly with the lapping of the water. Above, the pollard willows shed their feathers and the miniature gardens of wind-blown and bird-sown plants in their crowns look strangely exposed amid the naked boughs.

Without warning, this subdued late-autumn scene is transformed. Like a speeding arrow, a kingfisher sweeps into view between the outermost willow wands and the silvery water, piercing the scene with its brilliant turquoise wings and orange body. It is gone in the twinkling of an eye but the memory of its fleeting appearance bestows a warm glow on the dying afternoon.

6 November 1982

SPRINGS abound along the ridge of the wolds upon which our village stands. The many streams whose origins can be traced from these water-issues have played a considerable part in the shaping of our landscape on their short journey to swell the River Windrush.

The source of one such stream is located above the village, where the water cascades into a stone trough before being piped under the nearby road and thence down the slope towards the valley. This trough, once a source of refreshment for passing horses, is now passed by unnoticed. Sheltered by the hedge, its outline is softened by a covering of moss and lichens, and in summer this growth is added to by the ferny leaves and red flowers of herb Robert.

Beyond my garden hedge, the stream emerges to pursue a tortuous course through the sloping fields on the west of the village. It seems that its tiny valley was used as a boundary when the fields came into being, for the enclosures follow its line down towards the valley.

This modest stream is a lifeline for wild creatures during severe weather. Its snowy margins are covered with tiny footprints; even at times of extreme cold there is a constant supply of running water and exposed mud to ensure their survival.

Though little more than a ditch for much of its course, this stream has rewarded me with some memorable sightings over the years. I once watched an immaculate grey wagtail dabbling in its shallow waters. Goldfinches and linnets feed on the thistles on its banks. And it provides excellent bathing facilities for a host of common birds in the heat of summer — a cheering thought on a bleak winter's day.

19 February 1983

ONE OF my favourite Cotswold streams, a tributary of the River Windrush, is credited with no name on the Ordnance Survey maps.

Yet in the four or so miles of its course, from its source high on the wolds to its confluence with the youthful river to which it contributes its waters, this modest nameless stream, together with another anonymous watercourse with which it unites, carves out a miniature valley of sheer delight.

Apart from one solitary farm, no human settlement exists along the stream until it nears its destination. This has not always been the case however, for traces still remain — in the form of mounds and hollows in the fields — of two villages which once existed within three miles of each other until medieval times.

It is tempting to speculate what brought about the decline and eventual disappearance of these little communities. A combination of disease and changes in land-use may have been responsible. At all events, a shortage of water cannot have been the cause.

It is possible, by means of a series of footpaths and minor roads, to follow the stream for much of its short eventful course. Woodland lines its steeply shelving banks for a good deal of the way and judging by the variety of the ground flora, this has always been the case. Dog's mercury, wood anemone and wood sorrel are predominant under the ashes, many of which are gnarled veterans. Polypody fern sprouts from their mossy boles, male fern thrives on the woodland floor, and hart's tongue makes lush growth in shady crevices under the banks. Lichens too, flourish in the damp shade.

It is not until the stream nears the site of the second lost village that it meets a metalled road, which crosses it by a ford with a tiny footbridge alongside. Here, by the damp margins, grow water forget-me-not and brooklime, and keen eyes can spot tiny water shrimps scurrying in the current to the safety of water-worn boulders lodged in the fine grit of the stream bed.

3 May 1986

BELOW WITNEY, the Windrush is scarcely recognisable as the river we know in the purity of its Cotswold youth.

Its banks lined with industrial and housing estates, its waters soiled and sluggish, it seems to burrow its way over the flattened landscape, anxious to lose its identity as soon as possible in the ever-nearing Thames.

Yet despite the featurelessness of this phase of the river's later life there is one small corner of the lower valley that possesses treasure of a very special kind at this time of year. On the edge of a certain village, where the sullied Windrush has been diverted from its original willow-lined course to flow darkly beneath a modern bridge, lies a fritillary meadow, saved from destruction some years ago by the far-sightedness of a local landowner.

Here, from late April until mid-May, local people — and a few privileged guests like ourselves — come to admire this nodding mass of strangely beautiful flowers. People of all ages stand and stare, or bend to get a closer view. Cameras are manoeuvred into close-up positions. The flowers are subjected to almost every kind of adulation — but never, ever picked.

Despite all this acclaim, the fritillary cannot be called an eye-catching flower, or at least not in the usual sense. The purple chequered blooms are quite difficult to spot at first and it takes a little time to attune the eyes to the search. Eventually however, perseverance is rewarded and a host of blooms appear as though by magic — some dense purple, others delicately pale, yet others creamy white in colour.

A close examination of an individual flower soon reveals the aptness of the description snake's head, by which name the fritillary is often known. The chequered markings on the tulip-like bell strengthen the resemblance while the shape of the flower itself reminds us of the origin of its name — fritilus, meaning dice-box.

The hour we spent in the fritillary meadow adds yet another delight to my Windrush memories.

2 May 1987

AFTER SHAKING off the last of the houses on the fringes of the town, the little river hastens on its northward journey to meet the Avon.

For the first mile or so of its uncluttered course, a footpath follows close to the bank — the haunt of the occasional walker or angler. Alders and willows crowd the water's edge, together with a scatter of hawthorns and sycamores. The bank takes the form of a sheer, if miniature cliff, adding an air of mystery to the modest little river as it gurgles beneath a tangle of branches.

There is one particular spot along this stretch of river where a meander has created a tiny shallow beach, barely three yards long, and the small boy still lurking within never fails to pull me up here for a few moments' scrutiny of the assorted items stranded on this tiny bank of silt and pebbles.

Fossils were very much in evidence on my most recent visit. The miniature beach was strewn with the remains of that curious curved prehistoric oyster known to children as the devil's toenail — some large, others tiny by comparison. I also came across belemnites in a similar range of sizes. These bullet-shaped guards of an extinct squid would have convinced me in my wartime boyhood that I had located the site of a secret ammunition dump.

Bones too, were prolific on my secret beach. They ranged from those of sheep to long-since-devoured poultry, as well as ancient teeth of cow and pig.

But the most intriguing jetsam of all were the man-made objects. Fragments of pottery — willow pattern, vestiges of crude glazed vessels, earthenware of varied kinds — a miscellany of every imaginable kind of ware — and a few others too. The glass finds were mostly acqua in colour, with a trace of bright blue. I also came upon clay pipe-stems, tapering nails and a corroded metal button.

I moved on, but not before pocketing the most symmetrical — and bullet-like — of the belemnites, surely a better specimen than the one I found last, which in its day had taken pride of place in my haphazard schoolboy-like collection.

30 April 1988

Through the Woods

A BROODING stillness seemed to fill the wood. Rays of watery sunshine pierced the leafless crowns above, accentuating the gnarled and mossy boughs and throwing into sharp relief the distinctive irregularities of each weatherbeaten trunk.

Here and there stood the hollow, decaying remains of once-mighty trees, now virtually lifeless, their pockmarked trunks encrusted with layer upon layer of bracket fungus, gradually yet imperceptibly reducing the spongy wood to dust.

Receding patches of greyish snow lay at intervals on the woodland floor, criss-crossed by the blurred prints of passing animals —chiefly rabbit and fox. A scattered heap of soil and dead leaves revealed the spot where some animal — a badger perhaps — had scratched deeply into the leaf litter in search of bluebell bulbs.

It was not until I moved deeper into the wood and reached a clump of beeches that I saw any evidence of bird life. Here a party of great tits were industriously flicking over the leaves and devouring the minute insects thus exposed. Nearby, my presence prompted a scolding outburst from a marsh tit — a smart agile black-capped bird, flitting agitatedly from twig to twig in its ceaseless quest for food.

A tiny stream threaded its way through the heart of the wood. This fine trickle ensures that even in the most severe weather both birds and mammals can quench their thirst and therefore stand a fair chance of surviving when times are especially hard.

As I stood on the rickety log bridge, a tiny wren stuttered into activity in the tangle of ivy-covered roots by the water's edge, to be joined by a blackbird's alarm notes not far away. Looking up, I saw that it was a far more threatening presence than mine that had caused the panic — a sparrow-hawk was darting by on the lookout for its evening meal.

26 January 1980

THE FIRST severe frost of the season, following closely on the heels of heavy rain and blustery winds, played havoc with the remaining leaves, which are now drifting down in multi-coloured clouds to carpet the lanes.

I could not have picked a lovelier morning to visit a favourite mixed wood of mine in the valley of the River Evenlode, where the eastern edge of the wolds meets the gentle elevated landscape of the midland shires. Here, clayey vales replace our limestone valleys and softer contours take over from the grey-ribbed features of our true Cotswold scene.

This tract of woodland was once part of the great forest of Wychwood — hunted by kings in centuries past and still retaining something of its former splendour despite the depredations of recent times. Here, mighty oaks extend their spreading boughs over a tangled undergrowth of hazel, dogwood, thorn and bramble, and the silver of the tall birches catches the morning sunshine. The golden birch tresses are falling fast by now but the 'Lady of the Woods' still keeps her grace as the fine tracery of birch twigs stand out against a sky of pure azure.

Even in decay the birch has plenty to interest the curious. The upper sections of the decaying trunks are riddled with the excavation holes of tits and woodpeckers, while below it is possible to study the spiky growths known as witches' brooms, caused by the activities of a species of gall-producing wasp. Another feature peculiar to the birch is the white bracket fungus, polyporus betulimus — a corky-textured parasite said to have been used for stropping razors in bygone times.

But it was to the oaks that my attention soon returned, for a scuffle in the nearby leaves revealed a grey squirrel, eyeing me warily — an acorn clasped within its claws.

8 November 1980

83

ALWAYS DAMP, even during the driest of summers, the woodland ride was a quagmire after the recent deluge. Dark pools had collected beneath the birches and the odour of damp vegetation pervaded the air to the exclusion of the usual familiar woodland smells.

Although the rain clouds had moved on during the afternoon, to be replaced by watery and intermittent sunshine, the dusk chorus proved to be a subdued affair and when the sun finally sank in an elongated coppery glow on the western horizon, a song thrush and a robin held the stage unchallenged as the shadows of dusk settled over the trees.

It was not until I had reached the edge of the wood, and had paused to admire a clump of greater stitchwort, whose star-like flowers glowed strangely in the failing light, that I heard the sound I had been listening for. Or rather, two sounds — the first a low quack-like double note, the second a louder higher-pitched call, also twin-syllabled yet so different from the first that it appears to come from another bird.

And now, as I looked up, the bird I sought veered into view between the darkening trees. Stoutly built, flying on rounded wings, with its long bill poised downwards — the woodcock beat his solitary way, patrolling his territory as is his habit at dawn and dusk throughout the breeding season.

For woodcocks, being essentially wading birds, have a distinct preference for wet woodland, which provides an ample supply of worms and insect larvae, which they obtain by probing deep into the soft earth with their flexible-tipped bills.

Sadly, they are also game birds and the ancestors of my golden cocker spaniel were bred to put them to flight for the waiting guns.

13 June 1981

84

IT WAS late afternoon by the time I reached the wood. Pigeons clattered uneasily in the tops of the oaks as I advanced along the narrow path which threads its way beneath their trunks. Soon, the canopy overhead was virtually unbroken, shutting out the sun except for the occasional shaft which bathed the lower leaves in brilliant light.

Brambles sprawled across the path — a good sign, for the butterfly I was hoping to see favours bramble blossom as its main source of nectar. Honeysuckle too, was plentiful, clambering over the lower branches. Its presence lifted my hopes even further — it forms the insect's food plant at the larval stage.

Eventually, as I reached a clearing, the first butterflies came into view. Close inspection revealed them to be speckled woods and ringlets — a welcome and attractive sight but not the object of my search on this occasion. I pressed on.

Soon the oaks thinned out and the canopy became less extensive. Hazel coppice and a patch of blackthorn thicket took over — not the type of habitat to favour my coveted butterfly. I paused, wondering whether to retrace my steps to the clearing, which matched the kind of spot likely to provide a glimpse of the insect I sought.

On the point of turning I noticed a flutter of wings immediately ahead. Advancing cautiously, I discovered that the path dipped to cross a tiny woodland stream and the margins consisted of swampy ground. The wings I had seen were indeed those of the butterfly that was the object of my quest — the lovely and all too rare white admiral — which had alighted on the swampy patch and had begun to gyrate slowly with open wings, oblivious to my presence, before suddenly spiralling upwards to disappear from view in the treetops.

1 August 1981

THE GRASSY clearing on the fringe of the woods has undergone a considerable change since my last visit.

One of my happiest hunting grounds for wild flowers and their attendant butterflies some years ago, it is now being steadily eroded away by the combined efforts of human industry and natural regeneration. The relentless plough nibbles away at one extremity, while further encroachment in the form of worn-out farm machinery offends the eye and endangers the unwarily-placed limb.

Yet paradoxically, it is man's inactivity which poses the greatest threat to this botanically-rich corner by a tract of Cotswold woodland. For since the recluse who once inhabited this spot finally gave up the unequal struggle some twenty years ago, the onward march of blackthorn and hawthorn scrub has gone ahead with steady and inevitable pace, engulfing the deserted caravan and hen coops and reclaiming the clearing.

It remains only for the ashes to complete the process. Already their seedlings are climbing above the tangle of low vegetation. In a few more years, sturdy ash saplings will bristle by the hundred over this former clearing and all trace of the old order will have been erased.

A rapid count of the species of flowering plants still holding on in this shrinking patch of woodland clearing gave some reassurance. A few spotted orchids were dotted around and scabious, knapweed, dog rose and clover were all in flower. Among the butterflies, I recorded meadow brown, wall brown, large skipper and small tortoiseshell.

As though to compensate for the loss of the other flowers I had come in the hope of seeing, a nightingale treated me to a brief foretaste of its nocturne before I set off back for home. Nightingales have maintained a precarious claw-hold in this corner of the Cotswold fringe ever since I first came here. Perhaps they will benefit from the spreading low cover that the scrub provides as it advances over my dwindling little woodland clearing.

26 June 1982

Through the Woods

THE WOOD was brimming with insect life. Shafts of sunlight spotlighted basking flies on leaves, twigs and tree trunks. Others criss-crossed the ride ahead while yet others scurried, crawled or maintained a motionless pose according to their individual modes of life.

There was insect food in plenty for the predators in the heat of the afternoon. Webs of pure gossamer were everywhere in the low vegetation, while high above, restlessly active in leafy layers of the enclosing canopy, tits and warblers kept up their ceaseless labours.

On the woodland floor, the world of that most prolific insect, the ant, was revealed. On inspection, an antheap proved to be a seething mass of bodies, with a steady stream of other ants coming and going in all directions yet with the common purpose that we associate with this unique social insect. The path ahead was literally alive with these scurrying creatures, some labouring singly, others co-operating in pairs or groups to propel an assortment of booty back to their fortress.

Leaves, twigs, litter, animal remains — more often than not bigger than the ants themselves — were being conveyed in this fashion, with each individual insect toiling for the common good. Little wonder that many eminent men have been struck by the impressive achievements of this highly-successful tiny creature, which has evolved a social order of a remarkably complex kind.

After watching such intense activity, it was a relief to turn to the butterflies — colourful insects living at a more sedate tempo. The first of the speckled woods were fluttering along the rides — a reminder of summer's steady advance — and an insect with distinct preferences as far as habitat is concerned. The dappled path was exactly to its liking and the sunshine brought out these engaging butterflies in good numbers.

By contrast, a newly-emerged buff-tip moth, resting on a bramble leaf, bore a striking resemblance to a broken stick.

16 June 1984

THE WOOD where I heard my first chiffchaff last year has been transformed. Great swathes have been cut in the ranks of fir and spruce by the narrow woodland lane. Now, where the almost solid wall of trees once stood, stacks of sawn timber lie awaiting collection. Light has been let into dark, once secret places and the advancing year will see a carpet of flowers quickly cover the exposed ground.

The demise of the conifers was to be expected. They are grown as a cash crop, part of an economic forestry programme. The beech saplings which benefited from the cover they provided will now flourish and offer a longer-lasting and infinitely richer woodland in due course.

Sad to say, other trees have been swept away as a result of this wholesale felling programme. These include several fine old ashes, creaky and contorted with age, and numerous sycamores, oaks and hawthorns, all of which added welcome variety if not economic value to the wood.

Some recompense at least was provided by this drastic felling. Two old tree stumps, barely visible for the crowding conifers, can now be inspected at leisure and I am hoping that they will be spared indefinitely for they not only represent the nature of the old woodland that once flourished here but in their advanced stage of decay serve as hosts to a variety of fascinating plant life.

The first of these relics of the old woodland is a low stump of considerable girth, covered by a thick mantle of moss, from which common polypody fern, wood sorrel, herb Robert and a mixture of small plants sprout in profusion. The second remnant is the hollow shell of an unidentifiable tree, riddled with holes and stripped of every vestige of bark. Squirrels have stored their winter hoard within its ravaged interior and mice have strewn litter over its crumbling floor.

My pleasure at finding the remains of the old trees made up for the non-appearance of the chiffchaff. Perhaps he will have returned when next I come this way.

5 April 1986

I HAD imagined that I had explored all the paths criss-crossing the wood but on this occasion I found myself on unfamiliar ground.

Wide and welcoming at first, this new path soon began to dip sharply, leaving the flora-rich mixed woodland to plunge on an obscure course through a clump of ashes and towards a dense belt of spruce trees near the extremity of the wood.

Just before reaching the spruces, I found my path blocked by a fallen ash, forcing me to make a detour over rough ground carpeted with dog's mercury, bluebells and coarse grass, in which snapped off branches from the fallen ash were half-concealed. I had almost completed the diversion when I noticed a plant with four pointed oval leaves topped by a spidery flower of yellowish-green petals. This flower had a purplish-black centre and was instantly recognisable as the herb paris — once fairly common in damp limestone woodland but nowadays rather more sparing in its distribution.

Having accidentally found one specimen, I made a systematic search and was delighted at coming across twenty or so more nearby, indicating that the plant is at present in no danger of disappearing from the area — one in which, over 50 years ago, it was recorded by H. J. Massingham in the very same wood. In 'Wold Without End', he referred to its 'formal geometry' — a feature to which the herb paris owes its unusual name, derived from the Latin pares, meaning equal, said to refer to the symmetry of its parts.

The spidery resemblance of the flower arises from the arrangement of the petals and sepals radiating from the shiny flower hub. This pattern may have also accounted for the local names by which the herb paris is known — lover's knot and true lover's knot.

4 June 1988

DURING MAY, when following the track through the wood, I had paused to admire the flowers of the wild strawberry scattered along the bank.

Today, two months later, I returned to engage in a solitary pick-your-own session, gathering handfuls of the tiny bright red globes hanging among the grasses. There had been rain earlier, and each fruit bore a single droplet, which seemed to enhance the taste.

Wild strawberries possess a flavour totally unlike their cultivated counterparts. True, a good picking is needed to fill a punnet but the search is well worthwhile, especially as it often results in the finding of some of the less conspicuous wild flowers that may otherwise have escaped detection.

Today was no exception. I was constantly diverted from my fruit-picking by the discovery of patches of milkwort, self-heal, and white bedstraw, with here and there a clump of marjoram or St. John's wort, or a solitary pale orchid half-hidden in the burgeoning vegetation.

The character of the woodland changes towards its southern extremity and this in turn affects the nature of the track. From being a wide grassy ride climbing between spaced trees with a broken canopy overhead, it changes into a dark narrow way, burrowing beneath a tangle of dense foliage as it wriggles down into the valley.

This is the haunt of badgers, which have used the path, like man, for countless generations. Their side tracks branch off boldly at intervals, their scratchings and diggings mark the track margins, and occasionally the passing walker gets an unmistakable whiff of the elusive nocturnal mammal as the subdued light begins to fade.

No wild strawberries tempt one to linger here. In fact it is something of a relief to leave the wood by the stile and to emerge on the lane flanking the little valley.

Below, the stream that forms a headwater of the Windrush gurgles its half-hidden way beneath lush banks and mossy stumps, splashing silver at intervals in gaps between the trees, where thirsty yet methodical badgers have worn another secret path.

23 July 1988

Birds and Beasts

A DISTINCTIVE feature of late afternoons in September is the appearance of flocks of starlings. The swish of their wings can be clearly heard as they pass rapidly overhead, bound for a large communal roost somewhere across the valley.

The ubiquitous starling has few admirers. Prolific, adaptable and garrulous, starlings are branded as carriers of disease and are persecuted for fouling and damaging city buildings. They are generally unwelcome at bird tables and seldom feature with robins, wrens, tits and the other familiar garden birds on our Christmas cards. In fact apart from allowing a little grudging respect for their success, most people tend to regard the starling as something of a villain.

At this time of year however, starlings perform a valuable service both to farmer and gardener. Family groups and flocks of varying size descend suddenly on fields and lawns in search of emerging craneflies, which they devour in great quantities. At the larval stage, these insects are a notorious pest, feeding voraciously on the roots of vegetable crops, so the starlings' depredations ensure that their numbers are kept under control.

The starling's subtle colouring is another redeeming feature. A mixture of bronze, green and purple tints earlier in the year, the plumage acquires an attractive spotted quality in winter, when our native population is augmented by flocks from northern Europe.

In the meantime, I am pleased to see the industrious starlings invading my lawn, and enjoy watching the brownish-coloured juveniles perfecting their cranefly-catching techniques in the September sunshine.

15 September 1979

THE CARRION crow was searching for food on a large open grassy field when the cat approached. The crow, which had just found a morsel of food, stood its ground and continued to feed, despite the cat's close proximity.

Suddenly, as the cat's unswerving course brought it to within a few yards of the crow, the bird, as though deciding that attack was the best means of defence, turned from the food and advanced boldly towards the intruder, its beak poised threateningly. The cat stopped, uncertain, in its tracks, eyeing the crow warily. A violent encounter seemed imminent.

This was not to be however. The crow, having demonstrated his defiance, turned back to his meal, leaving the cat still motionless. Now it was the cat's turn to take the initiative. Slowly, with the stealth characteristic of its kind, it began an outflanking movement behind the feeding crow. The bird soon sensed what was afoot and backed away uneasily, half-opening its wings as it endeavoured — or so it seemed — to keep itself between its food and the cat.

By now both creatures were moving in widening orbits around the food, which seemed to be forgotten as the tactical battle intensified. Suddenly however, the crow broke the deadlock by making off on outstretched wings, leaving the cat in possession of the prize, which it sniffed suspiciously and promptly left to continue on its way.

I too, continued on mine — grateful for the entertainment yet aware of the danger of interpreting what I had just seen in human terms.

24 November 1979

LIKE A giant moth, the barn owl flitted to and fro on silently-beating wings, quartering the waterside meadow and avoiding the scattered bushes with an effortless tilt of the wing. Never more than ten feet or so from the ground, it glided to earth at intervals, though without succeeding in capturing prey.

I was able to watch its methodical progress for some time until it finally disappeared from view behind a clump of willows. The afternoon was well advanced but dusk was still some way off. Hunger had driven the bird to hunt now rather than wait for the cover of darkness.

Happily the Cotswolds remain a favoured region as far as the barn owl is concerned. They nest in hollow trees, as well as in barns, church towers and derelict buildings and as the analysis of their regurgitated pellets reveals, they exist on a diet of rats, mice and voles, thus performing a most useful service in the countryside.

As with other predators, barn owls are at risk from high concentrations of pesticides. Toxic chemicals build up in their tissue and result in infertility and death. A further hazard they face results from the increase of motor traffic. Many hunting owls are struck by cars at dusk or in the early morning, as I have found on my travels.

In less enlightened times, barn owls were persecuted as birds of ill-omen. Many were killed for decorative purposes, often ending up stuffed and mounted in farmhouses. Together with other birds of prey, they were also destroyed in the misguided belief that they were responsible for depleting game stocks.

Today, thanks to widespread education and legal protection, the barn owl — symbol of the Gloucestershire Trust for Nature Conservation — is universally recognised as a beneficial and beautiful bird that must be conserved at all costs.

23 February 1980

ALTHOUGH hares were fairly active throughout March, I had to wait until the first week of April to witness an exhibition of the so-called madness for which these creatures are celebrated during the third month of the year.

I spotted four hares sitting fairly close together in a ploughed field. Suddenly one hare, obviously a male, started to run round two of the others in wide circles, jumping high in the air at intervals and once almost leaping over the back of one of the sitting pair.

The fourth animal, presumably another male, made what seemed like a half-hearted attempt to intrude in this activity, standing momentarily on his back legs and sparring, boxer-fashion, at his approaching rival. The sprinting hare made short work of the challenge, however, sweeping aside his adversary with a rapid spring of his long back legs before continuing with his frantic circling.

As is often the case with observation of wild animal behaviour, this incident ended inconclusively, with one of the females bounding off through a gap in a distant stone wall, pursued by the vanquished male.

My cocker spaniel cannot resist a futile chase after a hare. I am quite content to let him have his fling, safe in the knowledge of what the outcome will be. Relying entirely on scent, the dog makes off in pursuit of the bounding hare, which after racing across a field in a wide curve, suddenly makes a long leap, followed by a series of jumps. This trick baffles the dog completely and after nosing round excitedly, trying in vain to pick up the missing scent, he returns at last, utterly mystified, to the place where I am waiting.

12 April 1980

THE DUSK chorus, although less exuberant and spectacular than that which greets the dawn, is nonetheless one of the delights of April. I lingered to listen to this nocturne the other evening and was rewarded by two extra sounds as an unexpected bonus.

The three principal resident songsters — blackbird, song thrush and robin — were all in good voice as the shades of night began to gather, whereas the songs of the chaffinch, yellowhammer, mistle thrush, wren and dunnock soon faded away with the departing light.

Then, as I listened to the melodious trio beneath an ash tree, an indignant yelp of protest came from above my head and a little owl bounded from the branches on rounded wings and skimmed off along the hedgerow. This commotion prompted every garrulous bird in the vicinity to drown the chorus in a cacophony of noise. Pheasants honked, magpies chattered, chaffinches pinked and blue tits scolded.

Eventually, after I had moved my listening post to a five-barred gate some distance away, the noise subsided and the nocturne continued without further interruption. A scuffle and a series of high-pitched squeaks in the hedgebottom close by revealed the presence of shrews but this diversion was short-lived.

As the last light faded, the blackbird finally fell silent, to be followed soon afterwards by his relation, the song thrush. But the robin's last notes continued to pierce the darkness as I turned for home, by which time the first of the tawny owl's wavering hoots had sounded from the distant woods.

19 April 1980

EVERY open lighted window attracts its share of moths on these warm June evenings. Fluttering white shapes of all sizes loom into view from the surrounding darkness, as though anxious to compete with one another to hurl themselves on whirring wings against the light.

Moth mortality must be enormous. On our night drives they dash themselves against the headlights, disintegrate on the windscreen and fall stunned on the road below. They are preyed upon by bats, birds and misguided humans. Like the wild plants upon which they feed, they have been decimated by the widespread use of chemicals and pesticides on the land.

Yet moths still manage to survive despite all the adversities that come their way. Since boyhood I have always found them fascinating creatures and seldom does a summer pass but what I discover a species new to me or find out more about a moth I already know.

By no means all of our 2,000 species are nocturnal. The silver Y, for instance, feeds alongside the butterflies on our lavender in the flower border during the summer, while two of the best-known daylight fliers — the cinnabar and the six-spot burnet — rely on their gaudy red and velvet-green colouration to protect them from predators. The common yellow-underwing is also a diurnal moth and it too, has developed a way of evading capture. It makes use of its brightly-coloured hind wings to dazzle would-be attackers and is thus able to make good its escape.

The hawk moths were my favourites as a young entomologist but sadly their numbers have declined in recent years. What a thrill it was to rear them from the caterpillar stage and finally watch the imago emerge from the chrysalis.

Now I content myself with detecting nocturnal moths at rest. They spend the day blending into their surroundings — trees, walls, fences — even disguising themselves as twigs, leaves and bird-droppings.

28 June 1980

I RENEWED acquaintance recently with that intriguing little summer migrant, the grasshopper warbler.

Returning from an evening stroll along a bridleway flanked on one side by a cornfield and on the other by a stream and a tangled thicket of briar and thorn, my ears were assailed by an eruption of mechanical churring coming apparently from midway across the field.

I paused and waited, recalling previous encounters with this mysterious skulking little bird, which is so seldom seen, yet which fills the air with its monotonous reeling for minutes on end.

After making what I considered to be full allowance for the bird's renowned powers as a ventriloquist, I pinpointed the source of the sound to one particular area of the field and carefully lobbed a lump of earth in that direction, in the hope of causing the bird to fly. Silence followed, but no flutter of wings rose from the green uniformity of the field.

Still I waited, reluctant to leave without catching a glimpse, however fleeting, of this secretive little warbler. Two years earlier, my patience had been rewarded when I had at last spotted the streaked olive plumage and rounded tail as the bird perched momentarily on an upright stalk before disappearing once more into cover.

This time luck was not to be on my side, however. Failing light and continuing silence compelled me at last to move on, consoled to some degree by a particularly rich nocturne from a song thrush perched in a nearby ash bough.

But the hidden ventriloquist had one last trick to play. As I stepped back on to the road towards home, the reeling recommenced — as near as I could tell from the very spot from which it had first come.

16 May 1981

98

THE SOUNDS of young birds clamouring for food are a distinctive feature of this time of year. In the garden and along the hedgerow, parent birds are ceaselessly active from dawn till dusk, frantically trying to satisfy insatiable appetites and scarcely able to attend to their own needs in the face of such incessant demands.

No broods are more vociferous than the pale and speckled young starlings, pursuing their parents with open beaks across the lawn. No morsel proves too great for their yawning gapes as the harassed adults dig with frenzied concentration to unearth worms, larvae and succulent insects from the turf.

In contrast, the family of blue tits raised in a nestbox by the garden shed are being fed exclusively on a diet of caterpillars from a neighbour's orchard. Each round trip covers about 150 yards and the parent birds operate a continuous shuttle-service as a demand reaches its peak.

Little wonder that many of these helpless juveniles fall prey to the numerous dangers to which young birds are subjected. Cats are perhaps the most destructive predators, although traffic on the nearby road accounts for a great number, either directly or — even more tragically — by causing the deaths of parent birds on which these nestlings and fledglings depend.

Bird song, although declining both in variety and volume as summer advances, still gladdens the ear at dawn and dusk. Blackbirds in particular, have given of their best by now, and that best is just about as fine as any bird-song can ever be.

Two local blackbirds appear to have embellished their songs by incorporating snatches from our own music into their renderings. One includes part of a theme from Schubert's Great Symphony in its song while another, obviously less inclined towards the classical repertoire, has woven notes from 'Rudolf the Red-nosed Reindeer' into his performance.

27 June 1981

DISPOSSESSED from their long-established rookery by the ravages of Dutch elm disease, our local rooks have since colonised a tract of mixed deciduous woodland near the bridleway to the neighbouring village.

Two stands of tall ashes have been selected and the dozen or so nests stand out prominently in the tops of the as-yet almost unclad boughs.

A rookery in May is a place of ceaseless and raucous activity from dawn till dusk. The calls and conversational notes of the parent birds combine with the strident and persistent clamour of nestlings to create what to some people is one of the characteristic sounds of the countryside but what to others is an unrelieved din.

Despite their superior size, young rooks are just as vulnerable as other juvenile birds during the first critical days after leaving the nest. I was reminded of this fact the other day when during my evening stroll by the edge of the wood I came across a fully-feathered young rook apparently roosting on the ground some distance from the nearest nest-bearing tree.

The bird remained perfectly motionless at my approach and not until my hands encircled it did it withdraw its beak from within its folded wings and gape up at me with its automatic food-demanding response. Foxes, badgers and predatory domestic cats are all well versed at exploiting the easy pickings offered by a rookery. Indeed, the clamour of small birds' protests I had heard earlier from the far corner of the wood suggested that such a predator could well be prowling nearby even now.

I felt obliged to give my trusting young rook at least a sporting chance of survival. It uttered no protest as I lifted it and placed it on the highest branch within reach before leaving it to face the hazards of a dangerous world.

22 May 1982

Birds and Beasts

A SOMEWHAT uneventful walk in pouring rain recently was enlivened by an incident involving an unlikely combination of participants — a herd of Friesian cattle and a pair of pintail ducks.

Plodding through yet another interminal downpour of the kind that has been a daily occurrence so far this month, my attention was attracted by a moving patch of white on the sward ahead. A closer look through binoculars confirmed the presence of a fine drake pintail —normally an infrequent visitor to the locality — accompanied by his less conspicuous mate. This called for closer inspection, and I advanced cautiously towards the birds.

Approaching nearer, I now became aware of a herd of Friesian cattle also closing in on the ducks from the opposite direction. As I stopped to watch, the ponderous advance of the cattle brought them to within a few yards of the apparently indifferent birds.

With one exception, they drew to a halt, as though unsure of what to do next. One beast however, clearly felt no such uncertainty. It nosed forward towards the female pintail, which promptly turned, waddled hurriedly to the nearby river bank and plunged into the water. The remaining cattle now advanced upon the drake, which turned in consternation, wings flapping wildly, and waddled off in undignified haste towards the gravel pit, from which it croaked plaintively from the safety of the shallows.

This behaviour confirmed my suspicions that the birds were pinioned ducks from a nearby waterfowl collection that had opted for the wild life and had until now found this strange environment congenial.

Eventually, as the cattle resumed grazing, the drake pintail managed, with a mixture of stealth and speed, to scuttle across the grass to rejoin his mate on the river. Unlike the ducks, I had had a surfeit of wet weather by now and turned for home.

21 May 1983

THE MAGPIE rose from the sheep's back with a harsh cackle as I drew near and made off with laboured flight for the cover of a clump of distant trees.

Earlier on my walk I had come across the dome-shaped mass a magpies' nest in the topmost twigs of an overgrown blackthorn thicket — a prominent yet virtually impregnable nest site — with which the tick-searching bird had probably been associated, either as parent or nestling, a few months before.

Few birds have acquired an array of associations comparable with those of the magpie. Apart from its notoriety as a thief — Rossini's overture implies an impish hoarder rather than an out-and-out rogue —the bird's reputation tends to be of a rather more sinister nature.

In certain northern areas it was identified with the devil, and anyone seeing a magpie was supposed to cross himself, take off his hat, spit three times, and say: 'Devil, Devil, I defy thee.'

The popular rhyme beginning 'One for sorrow, two for joy', has undergone numerous changes over the years. The wording of the second line can range from 'Three for a wedding, four for a death', via 'Three for a wedding, four for a birth' — to the more recent: 'Three for a girl, four for a boy'.

The name magpie itself invites conjecture. The first syllable seems connected with one of the many variations of the name Margaret — the abbreviation Mag having been used to imply a chattering woman!

The word pie has lost its original meaning over the years. Assorted colours, rather than merely black and white, aptly fit the magpie's plumage, as anyone who has studied the bird's appearance will testify.

Magpie myths may be in danger of extinction through lack of usage but the bird itself continues to prosper, to the detriment alas, of many of our smaller birds.

4 February 1984

JASPER, the golden cocker spaniel who featured frequently in my walks and jottings over the years until growing infirmity deprived me of his company — is dead.

The severing of many years of companionship inevitably leaves a gap. Minor routines are missed. A host of associations — inconsequential in themselves — combine, as every pet-owner knows, to endear an animal and to cause a considerable wrench when the end finally comes.

From the young puppy stage, Jasper was required to adjust to two distinctly contrasting routines. Growing up with two equally lively children, he was expected to be the patient playmate, the willing companion in any manner of juvenile frolics — a role in which he excelled.

Out with me however, he found himself commanded to subdue his natural exuberance. He had to sit or lie in silence while I lingered to watch or listen. It says more about his innate character than about my skilful training that he responded so well, for I made many of my most memorable nature observations with his motionless form at my feet.

Freed at last from this restraint, he wasted no time in enjoying the delights of the countryside after his own fashion. Off he would spurt in a frenzy of delight, bounding over the fields until some scent captured his urgent attention.

Once — and only once — did the thrill of the chase cause him to ignore my whistle and disappear. He was waiting, appealingly contrite, as I returned through the gate, and submitted to the routine removal of burrs from his coat — a process which he hated — without a whimper.

Those carefree young-dog days have long since passed, but their happy memory remains.

27 October 1984

CONCENTRATING on picking my way round the muddy puddles, I almost missed seeing the drama being enacted on the bridleway ahead.

A sudden movement attracted my attention however, and I froze, though not before the stoat had sensed the threat my presence posed and had begun to take evasive action.

The little predator had been on a hunting expedition and had captured a rabbit, which, although scarcely half-grown, was far bigger than the stoat itself. It had been crossing the bridleway, dragging its prey, at the time I had appeared and was clearly reluctant to allow my intervention to deprive it of its hard-earned meal.

The muddy pools that had slowed down my progress presented something of a problem for the stoat, too. Not that it was concerned with avoiding them for the same reason — its sole aim was to drag its unwieldy prey into cover, but the mud made this task extremely difficult.

At last however, after much heaving of its arched brown body and flicking of its black-tipped tail, the predator managed to haul its mud-splattered victim off the track and out of sight into the safety of the tangled vegetation of the ditch.

I tiptoed to the spot where the drama had taken place, to find the clear imprint of the stoat's footprints in the mud. I bent down to examine the smeared trail left by the rabbit's body — to be met with indignant and defiant chattering from the cover of the ditch.

7 September 1985

SIX MONTHS had passed since I last climbed the footpath up the scrubby hillside, yet the going underfoot in late May was almost as difficult as it had been in the dark wet days before Christmas.

Wet feet proved a small price to pay for the delight of a rare fine evening, however. The distant landscape was bathed in a warm sunny glow, while nearer at hand, trees and bushes, bedecked in newly-unfurled greenery, took on a fresh substance, softening the ruggedness of the raw-boned terrain.

As I climbed the stile by the contorted old willow, its near-horizontal trunk forming a miniature garden of opportunist wild plants, a female sparrow-hawk came beating along the hillside ahead, her barred underside and long yellow legs standing out in sharp contrast with her dark upper parts. I paused to watch her sweep into the nearby wood, where she alighted in a statuesque upright pose on an upper bough.

Higher still, after climbing from the scrub on to the upper slopes, another predator appeared. It seemed that I had not been alone in watching the hordes of rabbits cropping the springy turf for a large dog fox emerged from a clump of elders and trotted with single-minded intention down the hillside, seemingly oblivious to my still presence a few yards distant.

Whitethroats and blackcaps were warbling their nocturne as I struck off for home across the sheep pasture overlooking the valley. Bleating sheep and their sprightly lambs scattered from my path on either side — apart from one heavy-coated ewe, which remained on a rough ledge above the track, bleating plaintively, her stumpy legs flailing weakly in the air.

It took a couple of hefty pushes to heave the helpless animal onto its feet and I watched for some time as it staggered uncertainly along the slope to rejoin its fellows — swallowed up almost by now in the fast-falling cloak of evening.

7 June 1986

105

CLOSE ON two years have passed since the death of the cocker spaniel that had shared my walks since the early days of my residence in the Cotswolds.

I have no dog for company now — except, that is, when I direct my steps towards a certain wooded hillside overlooking our local valley.

The house at the edge of the wood is the home of two springer spaniels of sharply contrasting behaviour. One greets me — though that is hardly the appropriate word — with a cacophony of indignant barking, while the other waits patiently by the open garden gate to accompany me on my walk.

Or at least, that is how it seems. For as soon as I am within a few paces, the ambling old springer trots out on to the path and, nose down, makes his way ahead of me into the wood, pausing every now and then to make sure that I am behind. Occasionally, if I pause for any length of time to watch a bird or to examine a plant, my unofficial companion comes trotting back to within a few yards of where I am standing, as though to enquire the reason for my delay. Eventually, having satisfied himself that I am about to continue, he ambles off again, making short diversions from time to time into the undergrowth along the route, but always returning to the path as I draw near.

Sometimes, when we meet other dogs and their owners, I am prompted to explain our relationship, especially when 'my' dog's effusive greeting is not reciprocated. Usually however, these encounters pass smoothly enough.

When the time comes for me to turn and retrace my steps, a single call is sufficient to bring my companion back. As on the outward journey, he takes the lead once more, before turning in at his gate to rejoin his partner, whose barking has started up again at our approach.

I wouldn't be surprised to learn that other walkers find themselves with canine company when they take this particular path. But what happens, I wonder, if they are following a circular route?

14 June 1986

Birds and Beasts

BUZZARDS have always maintained a claw-hold on this area of the north Cotswolds but this year has seen, if not exactly a population explosion, then at least a welcome widening of their range.

Early in October, while watching from my window the passage over the valley of a large and scattered flock of migrating swallows, my attention was diverted by the appearance of a large heavily-built bird, beating steadily in the distance on rounded wings. As I watched, the newcomer began to soar upwards in wide circles and was soon lost from view — my first glimpse of a buzzard without leaving the house.

But this experience — though novel in itself — was as nothing compared with my most recent encounter with this fine bird of prey. Following a country lane on the edge of the wolds a few miles from my home, I was able to watch at close quarters a pair of buzzards rise into the air above the woodland ahead. With upward-curved primaries and tails widely spread, the birds wheeled in sweeping arcs and were soon drifting effortlessly almost over my head, taking advantage of a thermal current to climb high in the heavens.

Here they were joined by another pair, which floated into my vision from behind the crowns of the nearby trees. I had to incline my binoculars almost vertically to trace the progress of the four as they receded into mere drifting specks in a cloudless sky.

I had one further unexpected sighting still to come. A fifth buzzard appeared low over the trees on my right before banking sharply on detecting my presence. This bird's mottled brown-and-white underparts were clearly visible as instead of climbing like its companions, it headed off on its slow flapping flight, interspersed with short glides, to cross the arable fields reaching away on my left, and to disappear finally over the rim of the wold.

Long after all five birds were lost from view, their plaintive mewing broke the silence of the afternoon — one I shall recall with pleasure whenever talk turns to birds of prey.

25 October 1986

107

I FIRST came across the badger path about three years ago. It emerges from the wood through a tunnel of bracken and crosses the narrow sloping meadow diagonally in an almost straight line to the hedge bordering the bridleway.

Although the hedge is well maintained and stock-proof, the badgers long ago discovered a way of passing through without attracting undue attention. This they effected by scraping a narrow gap underneath a horizontal sycamore trunk in the base of the hedge — a gap which remains unblocked when the hedge is laid and which is far too small to allow livestock to pass through.

Beyond the bridleway the badgers continue their route under a conveniently situated field gate and so over another, larger field, which dips down into the valley. It is not possible to trace the path beyond this point, although I am convinced that it continues — if not to the river bank — then at least as far as a set situated in a pocket of clay between outcrops of limestone near the valley bottom.

Evidence of the constant use of this path over the years is easy to come by. Dung pits are scattered under the herbage on the fringe of the wood, while scratchings by the hedgerow alongside the route reveal attempts to dig up nuts, earthworms, and other delicacies. Occasionally too, a few strands of hair are left on briars and thorns overhanging the entrance to the bracken tunnel by the woodland edge.

Badger paths are often of great antiquity, linking sets considerable distances apart. A gamekeeper once showed me a path which he insisted extended for several miles across the north-east Cotswolds. Ernest Neal — much of whose work on badgers was carried out in the region —has pointed out that badger routes are often used by humans as footpaths.

The permanence of badger ways has been acknowledged both by foresters and motorway engineers, who have provided special gates and artificial tunnels to allow these intelligent and beneficial animals to follow their ancient routes across the changing landscape.

21 February 1987

MY ROUTE lay along one of the little-used minor roads radiating across the Cotswolds. Flanked by stone walls, it climbed and dipped with the terrain and the bends at intervals served as a perfect speed-control.

Such a road is best avoided by those in a hurry, not only in their own interests but in those of the rest of us too. This particular stretch of road was deserted on this occasion, otherwise I should hardly have noticed the diminutive fellow traveller hastening towards me.

This was a weasel, leaping with great dexterity and singlemindedness along the uneven top of the wall. Disappearing completely at intervals on its undulating course, it bounded by in a manner which suggested that it was hot on the trail of prey.

Noticing a suitable nearside pull-in ahead, I stopped the car and slid across into the passenger seat, half-hoping that the receding form of the little hunter might still be visible in the wing mirror. Seeing nothing, I resolved to take a stroll back the way I had come, just in case the weasel was still within range.

It took but a few seconds more to extract my binocular case from the glove compartment, remove the binoculars, and slide the strap round my neck, ready to set off. Yet within that short space of time a glance in my rear mirror revealed that the weasel was once more in sight —returning the way it had come.

Motionless, I sat and watched it draw near and eventually pass the car, moving as nimbly as before along the wall top, apparently in no way handicapped by the pathetic bundle of fur — what appeared to be a field vole — held in the vice-like grip of its jaws.

I watched it until it disappeared — some forty yards or so ahead —and assumed by then that I had seen the last of it. To my surprise however, it appeared again several minutes later, no doubt on the hunt for further prey for its voracious young, but a passing car disturbed it and put an end to my entertaining diversion.

16 May 1987

The Green Mantle

THE GREAT beech hanger appeared to be on fire. The clear morning light combined with a frame of cloudless blue sky to transform the ridge into a vast expanse of glowing coals, thrown into even sharper relief by the great grey beech pillars rising aloft.

The feeling of awe grew as I entered the wood and stood beneath the mighty trunks, my feet buried in a leafy carpet. High above, the turning leaves crowded into an intricate canopy. Every vein and margin was accentuated, the great boughs divided and arched like the vaulting of some vast cathedral.

The silence reinforced the illusion. Bird song over for the year, no sound broke the calm. Not even a leaf moved in the sharp morning air. And yet even here, in what at first glance seemed a world of permanence, change, and its ally, decay, were stealthily yet inexorably at work. Closer inspection revealed that not only the leaves, but the timber itself, was succumbing to the ravages of time. Many huge boughs had already crashed down, and lay rotting on the leaf-strewn woodland floor. Others were pockmarked with holes. Yet others, snapped by the wind, hung on precariously until the next high wind completed the work its predecessors had begun.

The beech is aptly named 'Mother of the Forest'. Our Cotswold woods, like those of the Chilterns, are primarily of beech. Whether seen as an individual tree, grey and massive, with its foliage, as at this time of year, a blaze of glorious colour; or viewed in a clump, perched high on the wolds against a sweep of skyline; or as now, in a wood, tall and noble as to create the majesty of a cathedral — the beech is an integral part of the Cotswold scene.

These great beeches are past their prime. I must look long and hard at their fiery crowns for they, like their turning leaves, are drawing towards their end. Sheltered by conifers, a planting of beech saplings are thriving not far distant. The succession is assured.

10 November 1979

The Green Mantle

OUR COTSWOLD roadside verges offer a feast for the senses in high summer. Cluster upon cluster of meadow cranesbill flowers delight the eye, shimmering like a blue haze whenever the sun puts in a fleeting appearance.

More sparingly distributed, yet equally beautiful in its paler blue, the tall scabious rises above the tapestry of ground-covering vegetation. Its nectar proves an irresistible lure to bees, butterflies and day-flying moths alike.

Another July flower attractive to insects, the gaudy knapweed, with its tufts of purplish-red flowers, brings extra colourful variation to the verges, soon to be further brightened by towering clumps of rosebay willowherb, the uppermost spikes of which are coming into bloom by mid-July.

The flowers mentioned so far may play the main roles in July's floral pageant but without that unsung band of support-players the show would lack its customary gaiety. So let us give praise where it is due — to the clovers, vetches and trefoils, to the campions, to daisies and dandelions, docks and burdocks, to self-heal, with its sublime shade of blue, and to hawkweeds and buttercups and climbing, clinging goosegrass. For without these crowd-players, ubiquitous and taken for granted, our roadside verges would lose their delight and travel would be a monotonous affair.

Roadside verge flora varies according to adjacent land-use. The shade provided by a belt of woodland has a profound effect on the distribution of verge-flowering plants. Admiring a lush, species-rich verge recently, I noticed than when I left the open situation and dipped downhill under an avenue of beeches, the ferny-leaved Herb Robert emerged as the dominant flower, thriving under a canopy that other plants shunned.

Wild strawberries tolerate the shade too, and I forsook the flowers for a little fruit-picking along the shady banks.

19 July 1980

113

APART FROM a few scraps of rotten wood, no trace of the old elm remains.

When I first knew it — almost ten years ago — its mighty trunk towered almost a hundred feet above the furrowed upland pasture where it stood. Its widely spreading boughs provided shelter for the cattle, which had rubbed their flanks against its rugged trunk for countless years. Woodpigeons flew clattering from its leafy branches at my approach while in the evening a tawny owl would float from its lofty crown on silent wings to hunt for its supper.

The clump of nettles round its base offered cover for partridges, which rose on whirring wings to skim heavily across the undulating ground. Rabbits emerged to hop boldy beneath its shade, and once I surprised a pair of handsome fallow deer, which made off silently and effortlessly towards the nearby woods.

The giant elm bore silent witness to many changes over the years. The old ploughland reverted to pasture but the ridge and furrow remained to testify to its former use. In our own time, a power line suspended on pylons taller than the tree itself was slung across the landscape. Soon afterwards, as the clouds of war gathered, training aircraft from the nearby airfield shattered the peace by day and night.

And then, some five years ago, a lethal fungus, carried by a minute beetle, achieved in weeks what the ravages of time and all the impinging activities of man had failed to do in decades. The elm's leaves began to wither and the tree itself to die.

For some time its lifeless peeled trunk was allowed to stand — a gaunt reminder of the depredations of Dutch elm disease. Even after its felling, the stricken tree lay where it had once stood, while the agents of decay set to work upon its lifeless wood. Now the power saw has completed its work and a local landmark has gone for ever.

26 July 1980

The Green Mantle

I HAD walked the length of this particular bridle path countless times and at all seasons and was under the impression that I had identified all the trees and shrubs along its course.

One autumn afternoon three years ago, as I paused to admire the golden glow of a clump of field maple in a hedge rising from the bridleway, I noticed a distinctive patch of darker brown and left the path to investigate. Sure enough, this was no maple. I could see as I drew near that it was taller and more symmetrical than its colourful neighbours.

Closer inspection revealed a darker, rougher-textured bark, somewhat similar to that of the whitebeam — another interesting lime-loving tree found sparingly in the vicinity. An examination of the leaves and fruits however, ruled out not only the maple and whitebeam, but also the rowan — another tree to which this specimen bore a superficial resemblance.

I collected some of the coarsely-toothed leaves, together with a few small brown egg-shaped berries, which appeared somewhat dry and unappetising. Local people to whom I showed these were as baffled as I was as to the identity of the tree and I was driven to my bookshelf to solve the mystery.

My find proved to be the wild service tree (sorbus torminalis) — a relative, not surprisingly, of both the rowan and the whitebeam, and described as being sparsely distributed throughout wooded areas of England and Wales, chiefly on clays and limestone.

Since its discovery, I have made a point of studying the tree in all its stages throughout the year, from its budding and flowering in spring to its present leafless winter state.

29 November 1980

SAD TO relate, the ancient hornbeam which has been a distinctive feature in our local landscape for countless years, is no more.

The whining saw has finally completed the work that the tractor began, and the old tree has been reduced to a pile of logs and lifeless branches. Unlike the decaying ash, which once grew nearby and which is now but a flattened stump, the hornbeam will soon disappear without trace, for its roots have been grubbed up and any day now its remains will be unceremoniously carted away.

Hornbeam timber, as its name suggests, is among the hardest produced by our native trees. This specimen must have been a veteran of many years for although its decayed state was obvious for all to see, much of its timber remained sound and solid and the heap of logs and grey fluted branches testify to its weather-resistant quality.

Judging by the badly decayed state of the upper bole, this hornbeam had been regularly pollarded over the years, resulting in the formation of a hollowed-out area in which water had accumulated. As with other pollarded trees, such as willows and ashes, this hollow had been the centre of the decay, the process of which had been further accelerated by the tangle of weeds that had become established there.

I can only speculate on the use to which this pollarded timber was put over the years. The slender tapering outer rods were most likely used for fencing or trimmed for use as bean sticks but whether the larger limbs were fashioned into cogwheels, spokes and handles, as was the practice elsewhere, there is no way of finding out.

A few brittle stunted little leaves still clung to some of the severed branches, reminding me that I shall miss the rich green crown of hornbeam leaves on my future rambles along the nearby footpath. I lifted one of the heavy grooved branches and ran my fingers along it and over the close-grained sawn end.

An old tree's passing leaves a gap — not only in the landscape but in our affections too.

5 December 1981

THE UMBELLIFERER family form the backdrop before which the changing pageant of summer takes place.

The creamy sea of cow parsley along the lanes has receded for another year, its end often hastened by the remorseless cutting blade, but rank upon rank of later-flowering relatives soon take its place, maintaining that succession which ensures perpetual delight over the coming months.

Hogweed, chervil, angelica, hedge parsley, wild carrot, wild parsnip — all these and many more will play a prominent part in our Cotswold summer scene. For the persevering seeker, such less-conspicuous relatives as sanicle, pignut and sweet cicely offer their own special qualities, while for those of us to whom poisonous plants, for all their sinister associations, nonetheless bring a distinctive charm, hemlock and water dropwort can be added to the list for good measure.

Generations of country children have referred to the hollow stems of the larger umbellifers as kecks, or kex. Both of these spellings have ancient origins, with which the poets were familiar. Northamptonshire's John Clare favoured the former spelling:

'The ramping kecks in orchard gaps
Shine like green neighbours in white caps.'

Shakespeare, on the other hand, spoke of kex, so perhaps because of his associations with our 'high wide hills and rough uneven ways', we should make his version our own.

I recall as a child in Derbyshire hearing an elderly relative use the term 'As dry as a keck'. Dictionaries however, vary in their treatment of the word, some omitting it altogether, while others attribute its meaning to any hollow or dry stalk, or to the fool's parsley in particular.

Botanists point out the advantages of hollow stems to rapidly-growing plants. They are certainly sturdy, and will withstand winter's ravages. These properties were fully appreciated by children in less-sophisticated times, as those of us who can recall peashooter battles will testify.

19 June 1982

FINE OLD trees in decline make a pathetic sight, yet they manage somehow to retain a kind of dignity long after they have been reduced to gaunt contorted shadows of their former splendour.

I know of no more striking examples of this sad state of advanced decay than that of the avenue of beeches lining a narrow lane climbing the hillside above the infant River Coln, south of Cleeve Common. I was not privileged to know these fine trees in their heyday, when the massive grey trunks supported lofty leaf-clad boughs, but it is clear even now that their shadow must have spread over the road, providing shelter for the passing traveller in wet weather and the welcome relief of dappled shade at times of intense summer heat.

Indeed, a few of the less-afflicted near the bottom of the slope still possess vestiges of their former magnificence. A few healthy boughs still bear leafy twigs, which are losing their remnants of canopy now, the bronze-coloured leaves drifting down to join the scatter of mast, twigs and wind-torn rotten wood on the road below.

Whatever their state of health, beeches serve as hosts to an extensive range of wild creatures. Among the birds my own particular favourite is the nuthatch — a perky active little treetop feeder of stumpy appearance, yet every bit as athletic as the tits with which it frequently associates. Nuthatches have mastered the art of climbing up and down and in every conceivable direction along the trunk of the beech and being highly vocal they are comparatively easy to spot as they bustle about high above.

Jackdaws find the numerous cavities in the old trees ideal for use as nesting sites, and on one occasion I watched a pair of redstarts apparently prospecting with the same idea in mind, although I failed to detect any trace of a nest.

Predictably enough, grey squirrels find the old trees very much to their liking. A pair of these resilient aliens watched from their treetop drey as I passed below.

9 October 1982

118

THE TOUR of inspection of my friend's newly-acquired garden was almost over by the time we reached the elder.

If the qualification for tree-status stands at 30 feet, this monster almost justified the name. Its girth exceeded that of many a mature tree and its branches, untrimmed over many years, spread over both the garden and the boundary wall.

We surveyed this giant for some time, each thinking his own thoughts. My friend had devoted hours already to clearing and tidying his new possession and it soon became plain that — in the words of the football club manager discussing the future of one of his less-illustrious players — the elder had no place in his long-term plans. I could appreciate his problem, yet faced with a similar dilemma I suspect that the elder would have had the benefit of the doubt.

Few if any hedgerow shrubs can rival the elder for sheer versatility. Summer would be incomplete without an elderflower flavouring in our home-made lemonade. And with the passing of the flowers we can look forward to the arrival of the purple-black berries for jam and wine making.

Nowadays we tend to view the elder as something of a weed — a ubiquitous intruder in the garden or hedgerow. Its powers of spreading and taking over from its less-persistent neighbours have earned it a notoriety which is normally reserved for poisonous plants.

But in the past, the elder was regarded with a mixture of awe and grudging respect. Known as the Tree of Sorrow, it was reputed to have been used to make Christ's cross. Another legend has it that Judas Iscariot hanged himself from an elder tree. Even today, old countryfolk will not burn elder on their fires, even though it kindles well when dry. Medicinally, the elder ranked among the most useful of our common plants. Its young shoots were made into a broth for chest colds, its roots provided a cure for various internal disorders, its fruit was used as a hair dye and its flowers for treating sunburn.

Perhaps I should have reminded my friend of his good fortune in having such a versatile tree in his garden.

16 November 1985

I RECALL as a child gaining considerable pleasure from decapitating thistles.

Armed with an array of sticks, we boys would surge over the fields, flailing as we went, whooping jubilantly as the purple flowers or downy heads, according to season, spun into the air before falling out of sight amid the forest of severed stems.

And although a growing interest in living things — beginning with butterflies and soon expanding to include birds — led to a gradual diminution of this senseless destruction, a good many years were to pass before thistles lost their unattractive — even loathsome — image and began at last to win some kind of tolerance from a growing boy.

Most of the thistles I encountered in my youth must have been the tenacious creeping thistles which spring up wherever man allows his plough or hoe to rest. Like the dreaded nettles that kept them company, they were a constant source of discomfort to bare-legged boys climbing fences or searching for cricket balls, birds' nests or blackberries. Later, I discovered that, again like the nettle, the thistle had an affinity with butterflies, offering nectar to the adult insect instead of food to the larva. Having donned long trousers by now, the thistle had in any case lost its terrors.

The notorious creeping thistle apart, I now number myself among the thistle enthusiasts, and living in the Cotswolds I have a rich variety of these remarkable plants to admire. The smallest of the true thistles is the dwarf, or picnickers' thistle, abundant on the short turf of the high grassland, while the largest is the handsome woolly thistle, bearing its great globular blooms at head-height along the grassy margins of fields and quarries.

A particular favourite of mine is the musk thistle, which since late June has graced corners of rough grassland and disturbed ground. Its reddish-purple flowers are more often than not solitary and droop in a fashion unlike any of its relatives.

The spear thistle is another fine upright plant common across the wolds. Climbing up to five feet in height, it gets its name from its long spiny leaves which, like the stout stems, are covered with down.

Thistle-watching in other words, has become one of my minor pleasures during my explorations of the Cotswolds.

4 July 1987

120

The Green Mantle

THE OLD crab apple tree seems doomed to suffer an ignominious end.

I well recall first seeing it, perched on the brow of the hill in the hedge by the bridleway, not far from the stile which takes the footpath over the fields and down the slope to the next village. I could see, as I paused beneath its spreading branches, that it was well past its prime. Its contorted trunk was pitted with scars and the usual signs of decay could be detected where these wounds had opened out and exposed the aged wood beneath the cracked and flaking bark.

One such wound provided the nest-site for a pair of blackbirds during the spring of my first year of acquaintance with the old tree. The nest was cleverly concealed deep within the gaping hole, about eight feet up, and to my satisfaction the occupants fledged successfully.

Every spring, the pink-tipped white blossom lent a welcome touch of colour to this stretch of the hedgerow, to be followed as the year advanced by a swelling crop of fruit, which was to litter the hedgebottom and the adjacent path as autumn gave way to winter. I suspect that I was not the only one to give way to the temptation to pick up and take a tentative bite out of one of the largest and rosiest of this fallen bounty — only to spit out the woody mouthful in disgust.

I vowed to return later, equipped with a bag in which to gather the best of the windfalls to make into crabapple jelly, but was deflected from my purpose by other demands — a pity, for sadly, the old tree has produced its last crop.

The beginning of the end came with the heavy winds that raged early in the year. One of the two main boughs was torn down, blocking the bridleway and leaving the old tree deformed and vulnerable. The surviving branches produced foliage as usual, but their days were numbered and recent winds completed the task that had already been commenced.

Now all that remains of the old crab-apple tree is a pathetic split stump, from which the fallen bough hangs on sinewy splints — a sad end for this veteran of a Cotswold hedgerow.

4 July 1987

AS SEPTEMBER gives way to October, the last of the pale blue harebells nodding in the breeze will finally wither, leaving only small brown seed capsules to remind us of the flowers that have charmed us throughout the summer months.

Twice recently, in widely differing circumstances, the frail little harebell has been declared by groups of country-lovers to be their favourite wild flower. The first of these groups were amateur naturalists, many of whom had an extensive botanical knowledge. The second group were a party of ramblers, whose interest was confined more or less to a casual acquaintance on their walks.

These admirers of the harebell are in good company. Richard Mabey considers it 'perhaps the most perfect of all British wild plants', while the late Geoffrey Grigson advised us to 'Look at harebells as though you have never seen them before'.

I suspect that one reason for the harebell's popularity is its adaptability. It flourishes in a wide range of habitats — from chalk and limestone grassland to acid moor, from sea level to mountain top. It has been recorded at 2,600 feet on wet ledges in Snowdonia but is perhaps best loved for its colour, 'cheering the wayfarer as he toils along the hard bare road', as one Victorian writer puts it.

The harebell is well distributed in Gloucestershire, having first been recorded in the county by the historian Rudder in 1779. It is met with not only along the wayside but on grassy hills and other open spaces.

Local names abound. It is known as the bluebell in Scotland, where the English flower of that name is referred to as the wild hyacinth. Other names include thimbles, fairy bells and old man's bells. The association with the hare originates no doubt from their shared liking for open country.

Like the other campanulas, the harebell is a perennial, with five petals and producing many seeds. Its Latin name, rotundifolia, refers to the rounded basal leaves, which wither before the plant flowers.

We must wait now until next July to enjoy the sight of these fairy bells once again, but their endearing memory remains.

1 October 1988

Chiefly Children

SOME YEARS ago, when head teacher of a village primary school on the edge of the Cotswolds, I was given permission by the parish council to carry out a nature study project on an area of waste ground near the school.

The ground, which had once been used as allotments, had not been cultivated for many years and was rapidly returning to the wild. Sprawling patches of bramble covered much of it, while here and there, the land was reverting to hawthorn scrub, with young ash and sycamore saplings climbing above the tangle of low vegetation in places — evidence already of the long-term process of natural regeneration to broad-leaved woodland.

The children's interest and enthusiasm led me to develop our nature study into other aspects of the curriculum. Simple scientific observations and experiments were carried out, involving plants and animals. Our mathematics took on a practical approach through estimation, measurement and weather studies. Work in language and poetry was enriched by close and regular contact with nature throughout the changing seasons.

Similarly, art and craftwork benefited through patient observation and deepening awareness of the living world all about us. Trees and flowers, insects and birds — all began to play an important part, not just in our learning but in our lives.

Soon, we were planting trees. We constructed a pond. We made nestboxes for the tits and sited them in favourable situations. The older children surveyed the nature reserve, as we now called our patch of ground, and began work on a large-scale map of the area, showing the paths we had made and named and many other features.

My successor carried on the work after I left the school and it was a memorable experience to be invited back recently to see how the project had developed in the intervening years. The trees we had planted were now towering giants, the wild clumps had grown even bigger and wilder. The good work had been continued.

The little learning resource that had started all those years before was now also a valuable wildlife sanctuary.

17 January 1981

Chiefly Children

MY COCKER spaniel and I have had a companion on our walks recently — an experience from which all three of us have, I suspect, derived considerable pleasure in our differing ways.

Certainly the dog was overjoyed at having an eight-year-old boy for company. Here was someone prepared to throw a stick and bestow a leisurely tickle with far more zest and patience than his master.

As for the small boy, there was every sign that his wide-ranging if fleeting interest in all that went on around him was thoroughly genuine — evidence of that innate curiosity that lies at the root of all real learning.

Consequently, we paused to look and touch, to discuss and question, as the whim took us. We paid no heed to arbitrary subject divisions —we dabbled in science, history, geography, geology — even the specialist world of archaeology held no terrors for us, and as the interest grew, so the questions flowed.

Why were there so few birds around now, as compared with earlier in the year? Why had the mud in a cart-rut cracked into a jigsaw pattern? Why had some dock leaves turned red while others remained green? Why did the road to the next village wriggle for miles round the hill instead of leading there in a straight line?

Inevitably, the looking and questioning led to collecting. We started with feathers, were sidetracked briefly by clay-pipe fragments, graduated to pottery before finally settling for fossils, which, as we had no container of any sort with us, had to be carried home in hands and pockets.

Our young friend has departed now for his distant home, together with the choicest of the specimens that he was able to persuade his mother to allow him to pack. Like my dog, I find myself missing his lively, if demanding company — a sure sign that I derived my share of pleasure too.

7 August 1982

125

A CLASS of school children solved a minor mystery recently.

Concern had been expressed about the increasing amount of litter scattered across the school playground and around the premises generally and despite several appeals the problem had persisted. Although most of the litter, consisting chiefly of potato crisp packets, was strewn around in the vicinity of the bins, a considerable amount had been deposited literally further afield — across the grassy area some distance from the playground.

As this litter nuisance continued even on windless days, a group of children decided to keep watch and before very long, the culprits were caught — or rather spotted — in the act.

They proved to be three carrion crows and between them they had devised a highly successful method of obtaining the tasty leftovers consigned to the bins during the morning break. One bird perched on the rim of the bin and with its beak proceeded to lift the bags and drop them over the side onto the playground below.

The other two crows meanwhile busied themselves in tearing open the bags and devouring the contents, to be joined later by the third bird. Eventually one crow detected a bag with rather more crispy remains than the rest and promptly flew off with it, to feed in peace on a far corner of the playing field — thus accounting for the widely scattered litter.

As the children watched, a pair of jackdaws arrived with a view to sharing the spoils. The crows however, soon dispatched their smaller relatives, allowing only a small flock of black-headed gulls, which had been wheeling around hopefully for some time, to land and feed from the scraps on the perimeter of the field.

30 October 1982

FEW BIRDS endear themselves to us more than the wagtails and the best known of these — the pied wagtail — has a special place in our affections.

The children at a local school have their own particular reason for being drawn to this dainty little bird, for a pair of pied wagtails have chosen to nest in the school courtyard.

Completely enclosed by walls, the courtyard is virtually catproof and the actual nest site — the open shelf of an old woodwork bench almost flush with one of the walls — could hardly be bettered. The children have had to suspend their normal use of the courtyard until the young wagtails leave the nest. This means that the school gardening club's activities have had to be curtailed and the infants' water and sand-play sessions have been moved temporarily to another part of the building.

The children have been well rewarded for this short-term inconvenience, however. They are able to watch, through the windows of their classrooms and corridors, the comings and goings of the parent birds, which alight with laden beaks on the school roof before flying down to deliver fresh supplies of insect food to their hungry brood.

Little wonder that the wellbeing of these trusting birds, which were around the school intermittently for some time before selecting their nesting place, has become a source of interest and pleasure to the entire school community.

29 June 1985

CHILDREN are fascinated by protective colouration in the wild and are often quicker to detect the presence of creatures disguised in this way than are adults.

Shortness of size can be a valuable advantage in the search for small animals and this closeness to the ground — allied to a natural curiosity — enables the young nature-lover to discover much that escapes the grown-up's attention.

All of which serves to put the leader of a group of young naturalists on his mettle and so sharpen his own powers of observation, as I was to discover on a field expedition recently.

We had spent some time engrossed in watching the behaviour of grasshoppers on a patch of waste ground and were just on the point of moving on when my eye chanced to fall on what appeared to be a crumpled discoloured leaf lying across the surface of a normal healthy leaf of creeping thistle. I had turned away before the implication of what I had seen registered in my mind — a dead leaf resting on a living plant and with no tree or shrub at such an advanced state of leaf-decay within sight.

I summoned my companions and together we gathered around the thistle. To begin with the alert young eyes accustomed to spotting rapidly moving grasshoppers found this new challenge somewhat puzzling. As they saw it, they were being asked to examine a perfectly normal thistle, and detecting no movement were inclined to assume that nothing out of the ordinary was present.

It was not until I suggested that they looked closer at the 'dead leaf' that its true identity was revealed. It was in fact an extremely well camouflaged moth — an angle shades — at rest with its wings folded in to the body and with each fore-wing wrinkled in such a way that it bore an uncanny resemblance to a dead leaf.

We left our discovery in peace and moved away. No doubt it would remain in that position — concealed from predators — until dusk, when it would be off on its nocturnal wanderings.

5 October 1985

'WOULD you like to see our hedgehog?' my young neighbour asked. Following her round to the garage I was able to share the family's amusement at the novel winter quarters that the animal had selected.

Its hibernation hideaway was a foot or more above the garage floor, inside an empty cereal box, wedged somewhat precariously on a stack of old newspapers awaiting collection for recycling. It had reached its chosen site by climbing up via a stack of folding chairs — leaving telltale footprints in the process — and had extended the confines of its cardboard-box nest by tearing both the box and its paper liner, so providing us with a ready-made observation panel to view it in its dormant state.

My young friend gladly undertook to keep a watchful eye on the family's new lodger, which will be given a few extra comforts to make its stay as congenial as possible. I passed on to her the timely advice offered on a recent television programme — namely that underweight hedgehogs (less than a pound or so in weight) need an extra intake of food to get them through the winter. A can of dog meat is ideal for this purpose.

It is a pity that most children's experience of hedgehogs is gained from the sad sight of their mangled bodies on the road. They do in fact make excellent pets, keeping garden pests — snails, slugs, beetles and other unwelcome creatures — under control. They will also tackle any carrion that they come across on their travels, so that their role as scavengers also deserves recognition.

No doubt I shall receive regular progress reports on the state of the privileged hedgehog next door. It could not have chosen more sympathetic hosts for its winter sojourn.

15 November 1986

129

THE CHILDREN brought their find for me to see. It was a fragment of eggshell, carefully wrapped in tissue, which was peeled away gingerly to reveal the conical pale blue offering nestling inside.

They wanted to know the name of the bird to which it had belonged, they said — the usual reason given for such visits, and one which, more often than not is a polite way of finding an excuse to display a newly-acquired treasure.

I could have supplied the appropriate name and sent them on their way happily enough but we embarked instead on a discussion about the charm of birds' eggs in general and of this specimen in particular. They had given the matter some serious thought already, I soon discovered, so the opportunity was mine to develop their thinking even further. For what reason, I asked, would a fragment of eggshell be deposited on a lawn at some distance from the nest? A few theories were put forward to account for this and after reflecting on the strong protective instinct so characteristic of parenthood, we settled for the explanation being that the parent bird had removed the shell well away from the nest after a successful hatching to ensure that it did not betray the whereabouts of the nest to a would-be predator.

This led us to consider the hazardous life led by wild creatures —particularly birds — during the breeding season, and especially in a built-up area like our own. Wild birds needed as many friends as they could get, we concluded, and we had no hesitation in including ourselves among that number.

Back in their classroom, the children showed me a nest that had been brought to school and this prompted us to consider the incredible achievement that such a structure represented. We examined the materials used and discussed the way in which they had been employed to fashion such a substantial, safe and snug nursery.

A profitable and enjoyable ten minutes or so had passed by now and my young friends, naturally enough, were beginning to reach the limit of their concentration. We went our separate ways, having shared this happy learning experience — encapsulated in a fragment of eggshell found on a suburban lawn.

9 May 1987

Chiefly Children

MY COMPANION on a country ramble recently was a budding young naturalist whose powers of observation belie his tender years.

On our last walk, Toby's interest centred almost exclusively on fossils and we returned home laden with spoils. My young friend's enthusiasm for country things has widened considerably since then however, and we decided to strike out beyond our local quarries in search of new experience.

Like all good naturalists, my companion was well prepared. He greeted me with a spotter's book in one hand and a magnifying glass in the other and we set off on our long-awaited expedition. Our first stop was by a ford, where a tiny Cotswold river flows bright and clear over a pebbly bed. Toby's keen eye soon spotted a freshwater shrimp and we bent low over the gurgling torrent — lookers-in at a watery world in which a host of tiny creatures went about their affairs unobserved — except by those prepared to linger and watch.

Soon, after adding caddis-fly, leech and several unidentified insect larvae to our tally, we decided to move on. Both spotter's book and magnifying glass had been put to good use. The time had come to try them out in a different habitat.

We chose an area of unimproved Cotswold grassland — an open space accessible to the public and therefore well trodden. Even so, the steepness of this terrain added spice to our adventure. Butterflies were now the chief attraction and the sun — fleeting in its appearance earlier — shone brightly and activated a good number of species.

My young companion soon realised that stalking — rather than chasing — is the best way to get close to these elusive insects and we had good views of skippers, blues, small heaths and marbled whites.

Observing butterflies led naturally enough to a consideration of their feeding habits and food plants. We even got around to thinking about why open grassland offered a richer butterfly population than the scrubby woodland nearby before the time came to set off back for home after a happy and absorbing journey of discovery.

22 August 1987

PROUDLY the little girl showed me her ancient field glasses, retrieved by permission from a neighbour's dustbin. Complete with battered case, they proved to be in sound working order and will no doubt provide her with hours of enjoyment until she graduates eventually to a pair of modern binoculars.

As we put Corinne's newly-acquired field glasses to the test, my thoughts turned to the revelation I experienced with my own first pair of field glasses many years ago. I was some years older than my young friend at the time but the delight I found in their ownership was no less memorable.

My growing interest in natural history had just begun to evolve from the name-as-an-end-in-itself stage towards a genuine desire to learn about the ways of living things, and this precious gift of extended vision to someone with indifferent eyesight was pure joy. Birds suddenly leapt into view — their physical characteristics, colours and habits looming before me as never before. I began a long yet intensely enjoyable apprenticeship in the art of watching and waiting and the rewards came thick and fast.

Never to be forgotten was the morning when, peering through my trusty old field glasses, I was privileged to watch a field vole return to the grass-ball nest I had discovered and wriggle slowly inside, causing the fragile structure to vibrate long after her tail-tip had disappeared within.

On another occasion I entered for the first time the private upward-spiralling world of the treecreeper — a little bird whose presence even now lures me willingly away from other, more spectacular sights.

I wished my young friend well with her 'new' field glasses. Slowly and carefully she returned them to their case. What delights await her as she too, learns to stand and stare.

12 March 1988

ANNA DRAGGED the heavy plastic bag into school and we gathered round to inspect the contents.

She had been playing by the bank of the stream near her home and her keen eye had spotted a strangely carved object embedded just above the water line. Her find now lay before us on the classroom floor and the involuntary gasps of surprise it prompted revealed how impressed we all were by her discovery.

It was a section of a large ammonite, measuring about a foot along its curved surface and with a thickness equal to that of an adult human arm. Arranged at regular intervals around the perimeter of the fossil were a series of ridges, while the inner surface was decorated by remnants of the coils by which this relic of the earth's ancient past is identified.

Digging once more into her bag, Anna produced yet more examples — of varying size — of the fossilised creatures which inhabited our corner of the Cotswold fringe over 70 million years ago. In response to our questions, she told us how she had waded into the bed of the stream and located her ammonite hoard submerged in the shallows.

Other demands on our time — however pressing — were conveniently forgotten as we fingered, discussed and speculated on this ancestor of the nautilus which must have resembled an octopus with a sophisticated coiled and chambered shell. An encyclopedia informed us that giant ammonites found in Germany measured almost seven feet across but this statistic meant little to us. Instead, by projecting with chalk the curvature of Anna's specimen on the blackboard, we were able to arrive at the approximate size of our ammonite, which although modest by record-breaking proportions, impressed us considerably nonetheless.

Anna's finds fed our sense of wonder. Geological details — the role of the ammonite as a dating or zoning agent, its relationship with time scales and rock types — will follow later.

9 July 1988

WE HIT upon the idea of a 'Posterity Box' one day twenty years ago.

The caretaker of our Cotswold village school, having observed with interest the project we were engaged on — drawing maps of the village — had remarked that some old maps were gathering dust in the roof space. Donning my odd-jobbing clothes, I had accompanied him up the ladder and into the murky cluttered attic above the main classroom. Minutes later we had emerged, triumphantly clutching a number of old rolled linen maps, which were passed down gingerly to the eager hands waiting below.

Our finds were a source both of delight and learning. They were early editions of the large-scale Ordnance Survey maps of the locality, upon which much additional information — such as field names — had been recorded, presumably by a former head teacher. We studied them long and hard and put them to invaluable use in our own map-making project. This led to speculation on what other treasures lay undiscovered in the darkness above and once more the caretaker and I ventured up the ladder to investigate.

To the children's disappointment, our search revealed little else of interest. But at least it led us to the idea of filling our own 'Posterity Box'. From listing what kinds of objects from the past we would have liked to find in the attic, we moved on to discuss what things we could leave to appeal to those who would come after us.

Soon the children were at work — writing letters, making drawings, getting together a motley collection of ephemera — coins, tickets, wrappers, comics, toys — to fill the sturdy metal container I had obtained to serve our purpose.

We packed our box to the lid with newspapers, magazines, tapes — and photographs of ourselves — and everyone gathered below in silent witness as it was sealed, labelled 'Not to be opened until 2068' — and placed in the roof space. That was twenty years ago. The children are adults now, scattered no doubt, across the country — possibly the world. I wonder how many still recall their gesture for posterity.

10 September 1988

134